★ ★

The DuVal Panama Canal Series

And the Mountains Will Move

And the Mountains Will Move

The Story of the Building of the Panama Canal

By
MILES P. DUVAL, JR.
Captain, United States Navy

GREENWOOD PRESS, PUBLISHERS
WESTPORT, CONNECTICUT

The Library of Congress cataloged this book as follows:

Du Val, Miles Percy, 1896–
    And the mountains will move; the story of the building
of the Panama Canal, by Miles P. DuVal, Jr. New York,
Greenwood Press ₁1968, ᶜ1947₁

      xvi, 374 p. illus., facsim., maps, ports. 24 cm. (The DuVal
Panama Canal series, 2)

      Bibliography : p. 348–360.

    1. Panama Canal.   ɪ. Title.

HE537.8.D86 1968   386′.444   69–10086
                                                      MARC

Library of Congress   ₍3₎

To

The Railroad Builders Who Pioneered—
The French Who Started—
The Americans Who Completed—
The Engineers Who Contributed—

THE PANAMA CANAL

AND TO

THE LATE WILLIAM FRANKLIN SANDS

PREFACE

The entire story of the Panama Canal has never been told. So stupendous is its history that it can never be fully told. The best that can be done is to present a few high lights along the four hundred years from the conception of the idea to the opening for traffic in 1914, to depict the main crises encountered on that way, to describe the parts played by some of its leaders in arriving at the great decisions, and to trace the development of its government and the evolution of the plan for the ultimate Canal.

The story comprises four epochs: first, the building of the Panama Railroad, 1849–1855; second, the great French effort, 1879–1889; third, the work of the United States, 1904–1914; and last, the era of modernization which is now in progress. These four parts are essential to an integrated story of the building of the Panama Canal which will show how the idea grew through the years.

This work was written on the Isthmus while the author was on duty with the Panama Canal as Captain of the Port of the Pacific Terminal during the period of 1941 to 1944. Thus it was possible to obtain directly much first-hand knowledge, to examine numerous original records, to talk with many Canal builders, some of whom had worked for the French, and to learn about the Isthmus—its geography, climate, and people.

The great work of the French at Panamá has never received proper recognition in the United States for its true worth. The French contributions in exploration, engineering, and organization were notable achievements that became the heritage of the United States and served as a foundation for the success of the later effort. It was the distinguished French engineer, Adolphe Godin de Lépinay, who gave to the world the fundamental plan for the construction of the Panama Canal.

In preparing this work it has been possible to examine the

Archives of the Panama Canal at Balboa Heights, the papers of John Barrett, Theodore Roosevelt, and William Howard Taft in the Manuscript Division of the Library of Congress, and the files of the *Panama Star and Herald*.

I express my appreciation to all on the Isthmus who have been more than generous in their contributions and suggestions. There are too many to permit listing of all, but among those to whom I am indebted are:

Major General Glen E. Edgerton, Governor of the Panama Canal, and Brigadier General J. C. Mehaffey, Engineer of Maintenance of the Panama Canal, for their co-operation and encouragement.

Mr. John F. Stevens, Jr., Mr. C. A. McIlvaine, former Executive Secretary of the Panama Canal, Captain L. C. McNemar, U.S.N.R., Legal Officer of the 15th Naval District, Mr. E. Sydney Randolph, Consulting Engineer of the Panama Canal, Mr. H. H. Evans, Acting Superintendent of the Mechanical Division of the Panama Canal, Mr. Donald P. Bean, Director of the Stanford University Press, and Dr. Graham Stuart, professor of political science, Stanford University, for their reading of the manuscript and helpful suggestions.

Mr. George M. Wells, who, as a young engineer, served on the Canal under its three chief engineers from 1904 to 1914, for his reading of the manuscript and the suggestions which his vast knowledge of the Canal enabled him to make.

Mr. Arthur Raggi, a French engineer in the employ of the New Panama Canal Company from 1894 to 1904, who read the chapters dealing with the French effort.

Mr. A. V. McGeachy, editor of the *Panama Star and Herald*, and Major Ford Lewis Battles, Air Corps, U.S. Army, formerly of West Virginia University.

Special appreciation is expressed to the personnel of the Panama Canal Library and of the Executive Secretary's Office, who through many months were so gracious and kind.

It was Mr. Frank H. Wang, Executive Secretary of the Panama Canal, canal builder, lawyer, scholar, and authority on Isthmian history, who in 1939 first suggested undertaking this work and co-operated so fully during its preparation.

My sincere appreciation is expressed to Brigadier General James G. Steese, soldier, canal builder, engineer, scholar, and statesman, for his critical reading of the manuscript and for his careful explanations of Canal history.

MILES P. DuVAL, JR.

BALBOA HEIGHTS, CANAL ZONE
June 1, 1944

The endsheet of this volume is from a mural painting by William Andrew Mackay in the Roosevelt Memorial Hall, American Museum of Natural History, New York. Courtesy of John F. Stevens, Jr. Theodore Roosevelt and John F. Stevens are there shown discussing plans for the Panama Canal. At the extreme left stands General George W. Goethals, and at the right General W. C. Gorgas.

TABLE OF CONTENTS

LIST OF ILLUSTRATIONS

ISTHMIAN HEROES

Hail to those men who dreamt of mountains moved
That oceans might by water-steps be bound;
Conceived across the land a passage grooved
Through treacherous shifting rock and swampy ground.

Hail to those men whose steadfast hand and head
Directed shovel, dredge, and track, to rear
A peaceful lake from Chagres' troubled bed;
To pierce Culebra's ramparts, wild and sheer.

Hail to those men who wage unending war
Upon the ravening jungle's thousand jaws;
O'er slides and floods and plagues prevail, to bar
Relentless Nature's triumph of her laws.

Hail to those men on ship and shore whose skill
In tireless sequence plots unerringly,
Through tortuous ways, by island and by hill,
The silent path of ships from sea to sea.

Hail to those men who know each struggling hour
Of building; clearly see the present task;
Above confusing murmur, say with power,
"Not ended; let us ever build, not bask."

—FORD LEWIS BATTLES
May 20, 1943

PROLOGUE

The American Isthmus was the great barrier that interrupted the westward voyage of the early Spanish from Cadiz to Cathay. It became the scene of intensive explorations to discover a water passage between the seas. None was found, but the Spanish did discover the regions where the land was narrow, where the mountains were low, and where rivers traversed part of the distance—regions prepared by nature for the earliest travel routes across the Isthmus.

One of these regions was the Isthmus of Panamá—a land of distinct contrasts. On the Atlantic side the land is low and flat. On the Pacific there are mountains, with the continental divide running parallel to the coast line ten miles away. In the highlands, irregular peaks, ridges, and valleys predominate; in the north, large swamps.

The low mountains of the Isthmus form a natural path for moisture-bearing winds that give this zone one of the heaviest rainfalls in the world and a most prolific vegetation.

In the low flat regions there are large mangrove swamps; in the higher parts, the jungle. The swamps and jungle form luxuriant homes for insects, birds, reptiles, and larger animals and make the Isthmus a path of egress for many forms of life in their movements from the Caribbean to the Pacific.

The Chagres River valley penetrates from the north and meanders in a southeasterly direction nearly two-thirds of the way across the Isthmus to the highlands; there it divides, the Chagres valley swinging to the northeast toward its headwaters while the valley of its branch, the Obispo, continues to the southeast toward the summit of the continental divide. From the Pacific the tortuous Rio Grande valley extends northeastward until its headwaters approach those of the Obispo—a configuration that has made the development of trade routes there almost inevitable.

1

When Hernando de la Serna explored the Chagres and the Rio Grande in 1527, he opened a new transit route across the Isthmus. Although first used as early as 1530, it was destined to survive all other routes in Panamá as the gateway of Spain to the South Sea. Vessels of light draft ascended the Chagres to Cruces and connected there with pack trains to Panamá City, thus forming the most convenient means of Isthmian transit, later known as the river route.

For over two hundred years this highway was the treasure trail of Old Spain, as pack trains transported the gold and silver of Peru, the wealth of the colonies, to the mother country. The route became an index of empire. It witnessed the rise of an expanding Spain, served at the height of her power, and was the scene of incidents presaging her decay. With the disintegration of the Spanish Empire it ceased to exist as a highway of world trade, but not until the idea of making a waterway across the Isthmus had become firmly ingrained in the Spanish mind and literature—an idea that was passed on to other European nations, notably France.

Coincident with the decay and collapse of Spain in the New World was the rise of the United States of America. Although at first only a group of weak and struggling states along the East Coast, these developed an aggressive expansion toward the West. Under the impetus of that westward movement came the purchase of the Louisiana Territory and its exploration by Lewis and Clarke, the settlement and occupation of Oregon, the Mexican War, and the acquisition of the Far West—events which gave the country two coast lines and made the United States a Pacific power.

With the East and the Far West separated by great distances, by trackless wastes of desert, and by high ranges of the Rockies, the difficulties of crossing the continent were so great that travelers were forced to seek less perilous routes. Some migrated around the Horn. Many sought a shorter route to the Pacific Coast by way of the Isthmus of Panamá.

CHAPTER I

TWO STREAKS OF RUST IN THE JUNGLE

The railroad across the Isthmus of Panama will speedily lead to the construction of a ship canal between the two oceans, for a railroad can not do the business which commerce will require for it; and by showing to the world how immense this business is, men will come from the four quarters to urge with purse and tongue the construction of a ship canal.—MATTHEW FONTAINE MAURY, Superintendent, United States Naval Observatory, 1849.[1]

PROMOTING THE RAILROAD

When the westward expansion of the United States in the late forties of the last century required another avenue to the Pacific, the historical significance of uniting the two oceans and the commercial opportunities to be found in the settlement of the Pacific basin were recognized by three men of vision—John Lloyd Stephens, most distinguished travel writer of his day, diplomat, and explorer; William Henry Aspinwall, financier and founder of the Pacific Mail Steamship Company; and Henry Chauncey, financier—the three who in 1847 organized the Panama Railroad Company in New York.

Among the organizers it was Stephens who had widest vision. With a background of law in New York, of extended travels in Europe and the East, of diplomacy, and of exploration among the remains of early civilizations in Central America, it was natural that his active imagination should be fired with the importance of linking the two oceans by rail through a land he knew and loved so well. To this end he dedicated his life and became the founding genius of the Panama Railroad.

In 1848 the United States Congress, desiring to link the two coast lines of the newly expanded republic, authorized contracts with two steamship lines to provide services to the Isthmus, where their traffic would be connected by the river transit route.

[1] *Senate Report No. 1* (57th Cong., 1st sess.), p. 504 (Hearings No. 17) (U.S.).

The contract for the line from New York and New Orleans to Chagres was taken by George Law and was generally considered a profitable business venture. The other, from Panamá to California and Oregon, was taken by Aspinwall[2] in a move which made people wonder why a man of his standing should have engaged in a venture with so precarious a future. But Aspinwall knew. He did not expect much from the steamship line alone. In his mind was the concept of a grand transportation plan—a plan by which a railroad across the Isthmus would connect the two mail lines and make possible the commercial development of the entire Pacific basin, including China, Australia, and the East Indies, as well as California and Oregon.

At that time vessels customarily stopped at Chagres, almost within the shadow of the decaying ruins of old Fort San Lorenzo located high upon the mouth of the river. Here passengers were transferred to small dugouts, often when the sea was rough. With carpet bags in hand they had to jump into the small boats that rose and fell alongside their ship in swells, wind, spray, and rain and then had to land at Chagres in a dangerous surf.

Boats loaded with passengers were poled slowly up the Chagres, with overnight stops at small villages. In the dry season they ascended as far as Gorgona; in the wet season, to Las Cruces. At these points passengers were transferred to mule-pack trains for Panamá City—the entire journey across the Isthmus being always a harrowing experience of four to eight days. The slow speed of the hand-propelled bungos, the lack of food, the sleeping on skin mats cushioned with grass in insect-infested huts, the long ride on muleback, the exposure to sun and rain, and the frequent personal dangers, all combined to take away, particularly in the wet season, whatever joy there might have been in seeing the incomparably rare beauty of the Panamá jungle, even for the most appreciative.

Following their plans, the promoters of the railroad went to the Isthmus in the winter of 1847–48 on a preliminary explora-

2 F. N. Otis, *Isthmus of Panama*, pp. 16–17.

tion to get exact knowledge of Isthmian conditions for transit. Stephens, accompanied by Aspinwall, Chauncey, and James L. Baldwin, explored the proposed route, following the valleys of the Chagres and Obispo rivers to the continental divide, where they discovered a 300-foot pass, and thence down the valley of the Rio Grande to Panamá.

Deciding that the plan was practicable, the promoters then sought and obtained an exclusive concession from New Granada (later Colombia), signed in Washington December 28, 1848, which embodied many of the terms in a previous grant obtained by Mateo Klein for a French "Panama Company" but which was later forfeited on June 8, 1848. The scheme of the American company was based on the business proposition of eliminating the long journey to the West around the Horn and opening a shorter way to Asia, Australia, and the Indies.[3] It left the company free to decide whether the traffic way should be all rail, a combination of rail and steamer, or a macadamized road for horse power.

Armed with this concession, the company on April 7, 1849, obtained a charter from the New York State Legislature to construct and maintain the Panama Railroad. As the "body corporate" it listed James Brown, Cornelius Van Wyck Lawrence, Gouverneur Kemble, Thomas W. Ludlow, David Thompson, Joseph B. Varnum, Samuel S. Howland, Prosper M. Wetmore, Edwin Bartlett, Horatio Allen, and the three promoters. The capital stock was set at only $1,000,000, with the privilege granted of raising it to $5,000,000,[4] a figure amended on April 12, 1855, to $7,000,000.

Early in 1849 a large party of United States engineers under Colonel George W. Hughes went to the Isthmus to make location surveys. Accompanied by Baldwin they ran lines, the first stake of which was driven by Captain John Jay Williams.[5] The work

[3] Ibid., p. 18.
[4] Panama Railroad Company Charter, 1849.
[5] Tracy Robinson, Panama: A Personal Record of Forty-six Years, 1861–1907, p. 7.

of such earlier engineers as John Augustus Lloyd (1827) and Napoléon Garella (1843), besides the general knowledge of the long-used routes on the Chagres River to the Gorgona or Cruces trails, must have been of first importance in locating the railroad line, for it did not deviate greatly from the lines as previously explored and later adopted.

From the start there was controversy regarding the location of the Atlantic terminus—Porto Bello or Limon Bay (Navy Bay). The rumor at the time was that George Law had bought all the real estate around the capacious and protected harbor of Porto Bello and was holding it at a price too high for the young company to stand, with the result that Limon Bay was selected for the Atlantic terminus in preference to the older and better-known port of Spanish days. Be that as it may, the map and reports indicate that Limon Bay was the preferable location, probably determined by such engineering considerations as the discovery by Baldwin of the mountain pass at Culebra, only 286 feet high, and a survey of the coast line. The railroad route in general followed the route of the present Canal. It followed also the Hughes survey, except south of the continental divide, where it was located more to the west.

Under the leadership of the versatile Stephens and the realistic Aspinwall, the company then looked for engineers familiar with tropical construction and labor. They found in Colonel George M. Totten and John C. Trautwine two of the leading engineers of their time in the United States, who had done important work in Colombia on the canal Del Dique from Cartagena to the Magdalena River and were familiar with construction in the tropics and with the handling of tropical labor. They were given a contract to build the entire railroad.

The first plan was to start work at Gorgona on the Chagres, thirty miles from the Atlantic, a central position that permitted construction toward the Pacific as the best means of quickly eliminating the twenty-mile pack-mule trip from Gorgona to Panamá City, and later to build toward the Atlantic. Trautwine established his headquarters at Gorgona in January 1850 and began the final survey toward Panamá; but difficulties began to appear. He and his officers were prostrated by fever. The two river steamers obtained to ascend the Chagres to Gorgona could not do so in spite of their light draft of 18 inches. After a delay of four months it was decided to begin construction on the Atlantic end.[6]

A sensational event had occurred on January 24, 1848, at Sutter's Mill on the American River in California—the discovery of gold. The news spread around the world with great rapidity despite the relative lack of rapid communication, and almost overnight the Isthmus became the stop-over for the "fortyniners" on their way to riches, but more often to privations. This tide of emigrants on the Isthmus dislocated values and made fulfillment of the railroad contract with Totten and Trautwine impossible. It changed the nature of the undertaking from one based on long-range business planning to one for producing great immediate profits. Also, Trautwine, in his survey in 1850, had found previous surveys erroneous. These factors caused the contractors to refuse to carry out the agreement as based on estimates of the early surveys. The railroad then appointed Totten and Trautwine as associate chief engineers,[7] with Baldwin and John Jay Williams as assistants. Colonel Totten left for Cartagena to procure laborers, and Trautwine remained behind to start work with available help.

GETTING STARTED

One day in May 1850, a *cayuca* approached swampy Manzanillo Island on the eastern shore of Limon Bay. The island was low and flat, about a square mile in area, and covered with jungle. Bordered by mangrove trees from whose trunks and branches pendulous roots descended into black, slimy mud, it afforded a splendid home for alligators, myriads of sand flies,

[6] C. T. Lindsay, *A Short History of the Panama Railroad*, p. 8.
[7] *Panama Star and Herald*, Oct. 20, 1883.

and mosquitoes; but to the visitors in the *cayuca* it presented hazardous and almost impenetrable obstacles.

Two North Americans, Trautwine and Baldwin,[8] carrying axes and accompanied by six natives armed with machetes, jumped ashore. The natives, hacking their way into the jungle, cut a path for the axemen, who with rapid blows quickly felled graceful palms, clearing ground in what was described as the "densest jungle, reeking with malaria, and abounding with almost every species of wild beasts, noxious reptiles, and venomous insects."[9] They found it impossible to work unless face and hands were covered with protecting gauze and equally unbearable to reside ashore.

An old brig, anchored in Limon Bay and previously used to bring building materials, was commandeered as a floating barracks to afford relief from perpetual insect attacks. Returning from his Cartagena trip with forty natives from Colombia, Colonel Totten placed them upon this overcrowded brig. Life on board was not easy. Below its decks the vessel was "alive with mosquitoes and sand-flies, which were a source of such annoyance and suffering that almost all preferred to sleep upon the deck, exposed to the drenching rains, rather than endure their attacks."[10] These, added to the nausea created by the ceaseless rolling of the ship in the ground swell, finally caused the purchase of an old steamer, the "Telegraph," which became a more hospitable home for the railroad workers during the rapidly developing rainy season.

Along with Colonel Totten had come John L. Stephens, returning from Bogotá, where, as Vice-President of the Panama Railroad Company, he had negotiated and signed on April 15, 1850, a new contract for the railroad with the Minister of Foreign Affairs, Victoriano de Diego Paredes. Approved by the Colombian (New Granadan) Congress on June 4, 1850, it was the fundamental railroad contract.[11] Among its provisions were

---

[8] Otis, *op. cit.*, p. 26.   [9] *Ibid.*, p. 21.   [10] *Ibid.*, p. 27.

[11] J. L. Bristow, *Report of Special Panama Railroad Commissioner to the Secretary of War, June 24, 1905*, pp. 296–335 (U.S.).

sections requiring completion of the railroad within six years, granting a monopoly of transportation, including a possible canal and river navigation and provision for free ports at the terminals of the road, and giving the company the right to propose police powers for security of the railroad.

What kind of man was this Colonel Totten who had the responsibility of chief engineer? Of small stature, quiet and reserved, he had the fine qualities suitable for a chief engineer rather than for the go-getter type of general manager. Tracy Robinson described his chief quality as staying power of the first order. "His opinion once formed, there was no more to be said on the subject. Indeed, he was conservative to the last degree. While he was modest and unobtrusive, it would nevertheless have been difficult to move him from a position once assumed. As a military man he would have been an obstinate fighter. As a civilian he was reticent, plain, steadfast, just, and the soul of honor and honesty. He was a superior man without being great . . . ."[12] In short, he was the type required for such an effort as the construction of the Panama Railroad.

After Colonel Totten's return, Trautwine and Stephens left for New York to confer with the directors about plans for the dry season and to recruit more labor, while Colonel Totten and Baldwin continued the work of clearing and tracing surveys, often working waist-deep in mud and water, each taking turns while the other was ill. At Monkey Hill, lumber was dragged through swampland to build construction shanties on high ground. After two miles of location were definitely decided on, work on grading was started in August 1850 near the present Mount Hope Station.

Stimulated by the rapid increase in travelers and the desire for quick financial returns, the "push to completion" became the order of the day. Laborers constantly arrived, natives from Cartagena and Negroes from Jamaica, and each ship from the United States brought construction materials and mechanics who

[12] Robinson, *op. cit.*, p. 33.

hastened the erection of the frame houses sent from New York. As soon as frame dwellings were ready, the floating barracks were abandoned and men were moved ashore to houses nearer their work. Working in mud and water, exposed to rains, oppressed by an appalling humidity, and exposed to diseases, the men formed a fertile field for medical work by Dr. J. A. Totten, the railroad physician and a brother of the chief engineer. It should be observed, however, that contemporary writers did not mention what later became the dread of Panamá—yellow fever.

With Manzanillo Island cleared, the railroad plan decided, and grading begun at Mount Hope, the line was laid southward toward Gatun. There terminal facilities were started, a town laid out, and work begun on the station at Gatun, almost eight miles from Manzanillo Island. The location on the Chagres opposite a native village was convenient for unloading men and materials from vessels for the work of piling and grading toward Aspinwall. Although the total force in August was about 400 men, by December it had grown to 1,000; but the turnover was large, as many were lured from work on the railroad to more lucrative positions on the California transit.

Trautwine returned to the Isthmus in September and remained with the railroad until near the end of the year, when he resigned, leaving railroad affairs in sole charge of Colonel Totten. Returning to the United States, he immediately undertook a defense of the railroad in the press, predicting its "energetic prosecution."

By April 1851 most of the track from Manzanillo Island to Gatun had been laid. Over the lowlands in this section the railroad was built on trestles made with piling "full of pitch,"[13] which even sixty years later, when the North American canal builders excavated north of Gatun Lock site, were found to be sound below sea level. The original rails to Gatun consisted of flat iron bars resting on wood stringers, but these were replaced by wrought-iron U rails in 1853 and these in turn by T rails in

[13] *Canal Record,* Jan. 20, 1909, II, 161 (U.S.).

1869. The gauge adopted was five feet, for rail gauges had not yet been standardized.

Meanwhile work was progressing elsewhere on the line. Chief Assistant Engineer J. C. Campbell was extending locations toward Panamá, working at several points. Docks had been constructed on Limon Bay, permitting ships to discharge railroad supplies and laborers. Even so, progress had not been rapid enough to offer competition with the regular travel advertised in the papers of the day. For example, in a Panamá paper the advertisement of R. A. Joy's Transportation Line described the route of the mule-pack trains as from Panamá to Gorgona in the dry season and to Cruces in the rainy season for "passengers, baggage, and merchandise" on good English saddles with everything necessary for comfort. It lamented, however, that one of the greatest causes for delay and annoyance lay in the large packages "totally uncalculated for the transit through the narrow passes of the road" and announced that these "should not weigh more than 100 lbs., gross, or measure more than four cubic feet" and should "be well protected from the wet by tarpaulins."[14] Another writer advised all passengers to provide themselves with "good hams, smoked tongues or sausages, pickles, good coffee, and their accustomed drink; a good blanket, if in the rainy season, a light India rubber overcoat and leggings, also an umbrella."[15]

With only that limited system of travel on the Isthmus, it was natural that the progress of the Panama Railroad should become the byword of the day, with everyone looking for its earliest possible completion. When the survey advanced almost to Panamá the local press howled for passenger trains for "even so short a distance as that between Navy Bay and Gatun."[16] But that required more than wishing. So traffic continued by the picturesque Chagres, whose fullest beauty can be appreciated only

[14] *Panama Herald*, May 26, 1851, p. 3.
[15] E. L. Autenrieth, *Topographical Map of the Isthmus of Panama*, p. 5.
[16] *Panama Herald*, May 19, 1851.

from a boat; and by mule-pack trains, which frequently met disaster by robberies and murders when miners from California were returning with their gold dust.

Nor was the trans-Isthmian river traffic always tranquil. For example, on June 10, 1851, as the steamer "Aspinwall," with passengers on the way from Chagres to Gorgona, and the iron steamer "Gorgona," en route to the sea, were approaching a curve in the river near Gatun, they collided with a shock described as "terrible, breaking off and tearing away the guards of the 'Aspinwall,' bending and wrenching her piston rod, and nearly cutting her in two."[17] Although the passengers and officers of the ship feared an explosion, the ships were separated, and the "Aspinwall" continued on her way with an estimated damage of only $500.

FIRST TRAIN TO GATUN AND THE NAMING OF ASPINWALL

With less than eight miles of road built after more than two years since the granting of the charter, the confidence of distant investors in New York weakened, though they well knew the dangers of the work and the difficulty of competing for labor in a market upset by the feverish gold rush to California. The original subscription of $1,000,000 was about expended, and the market price of the stock tumbled. Work on the railroad and the terminal at Manzanillo continued, and by the first of September there was only one mile to complete before the railroad would reach Gatun, but that was through "one of the worst and most ugly pestiferous marshes on the Continent." The writer in the *Panama Herald* recorded his impressions of this preparatory activity as including, at Navy Bay, "the air of a Commercial City . . . . the shipping discharging at the dock, the large warehouses belonging to the Company, the houses for the officers and men, the machine shops, the splendid new passenger cars, all ready for the road; besides the number of freight and baggage cars building, and that have been built, the locomotive

[17] *Panama Herald*, June 16, 1851.

puffing along with dirt cars."[18] Meanwhile in Panamá City the people awaited the news of the first train with great expectations, in the general belief that completion of the railroad would be the panacea for all the Isthmian economic ills, the basis of a permanent prosperity, and a quick road to personal fortune. Many thought of the Isthmus as the cynosure of the whole commercial world.

The tracks to Gatun were then ready for test, and on October 1, 1851, a train of work cars traveled from the terminal to Gatun—the first Isthmian train; but it would take a little more time before passenger traffic could be stimulated, as steamers continued to use the Chagres. The railroad advanced, reaching Miller's Station, three miles beyond Gatun, about the middle of November—a month that for the Isthmus has been described as a month of northers.

Two ships, the "Georgia" and the "Philadelphia," with passengers from the United States, arrived at the open roadstead off Chagres but were forced by the extremely heavy weather to take refuge in Limon Bay, where the passengers were landed. The situation thus created practically forced the railroad in early December to haul passengers to Gatun—an event heralded far and wide, for it established Limon Bay as the normal port of call, forever replacing Chagres. In New York the confidence of investors was restored, and financing was resumed. Among the Isthmians there was great joy, for by the starting of railroad passenger traffic there had come at last the partial realization of the dream of Spanish leaders who, from the time when Vasco Núñez de Balboa viewed the Pacific, had striven for a highway across the Isthmus.

What the Atlantic terminus should be called became a moot question. The opportunity for naming it came on February 29, 1852, at the ceremony for laying the cornerstone of the company's new office building—the first brick building on the island, fireproof and containing a specie vault. It was a gala occa-

[18] *Panama Herald*, Sept. 8, 1851.

sion on Manzanillo Island. Railroad employees and residents thronged around. Among the distinguished guests were George Law, owner of the Atlantic steamer line and a director of the railroad; Minor C. Story of New York, one of the largest railroad contractors of his day; John L. Stephens, then President of the Panama Railroad; R. Webb of Manzanillo Island; and Victoriano de Diego Paredes, ex-Minister of Foreign Affairs of New Granada, who was then on his way to Washington as Minister to the United States. As Paredes had negotiated the railroad contract of 1850 with Stephens in Bogotá, he was selected to lay the cornerstone and to proclaim the name of the new city.

Introduced by Stephens, the diplomat explained his part in the negotiations and how elated he was at the progress of the road and the obstacles overcome and predicted early completion of the railroad, as progress was already ahead of stipulations in the contract. When he gave credit to the individuals involved in securing these results, at the suggestion of Stephens he singled out the name of William H. Aspinwall for honoring. Describing the new town as destined to become the "commercial emporium of America and perhaps the whole world," he proposed that "we call this town Aspinwall, as a slight homage to so respectable a person." He did not foresee the repudiation of this gracious act by his own Government, which later changed the name of Aspinwall to Colón, in honor of the discoverer of America.

Replying to this diplomatic accolade, Mr. Webb in behalf of the citizens graciously accepted the proposed name of the terminal city. President Stephens also replied, stating that "no name could have been selected more proper, or which would give more general satisfaction."[19] Dr. Paredes then placed in the cornerstone a copper box containing a memorandum describing the ceremony, a copy of the contract with the Republic of New Granada, a copy of the *New York Herald* of February 9, 1852, and a coin each from the United States, France, England,

[19] *Panama Herald*, March 9, 1852.

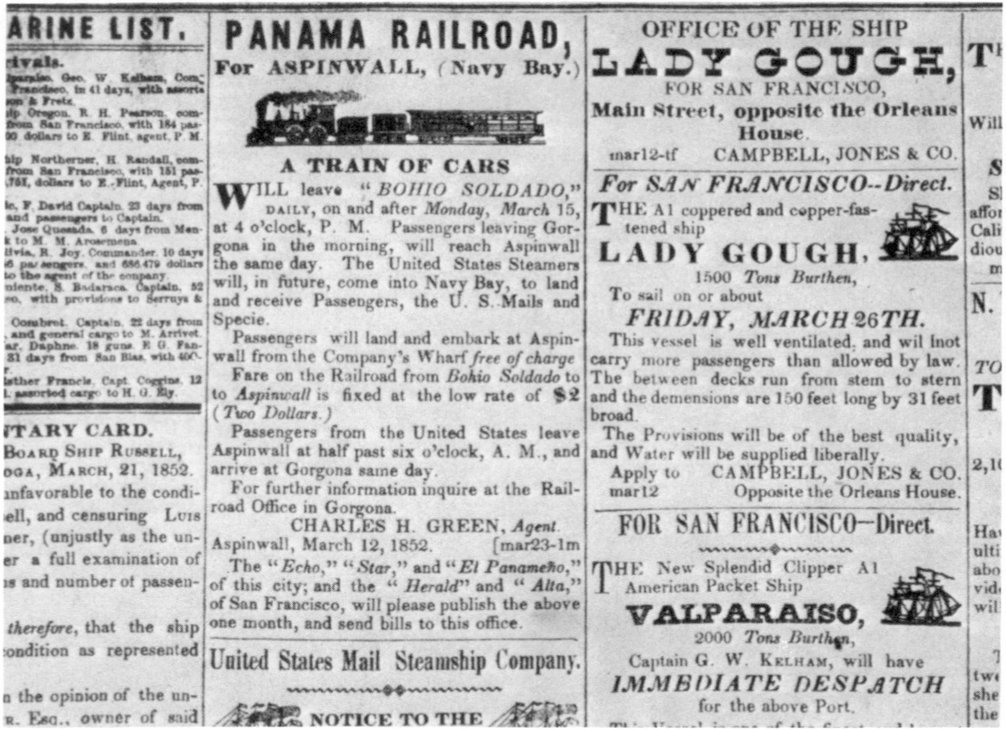

Courtesy of the *Panama Star and Herald*

FIRST PUBLISHED TRAIN SCHEDULE OF PANAMA RAILROAD

The Panama Herald, March 23, 1852

ARINE LIST.

dvals.

eamboat. Geo. W. Kelham, Com;
Panama, in 61 days, with merris
ses & Freigt.
hip Oregon, R. H. Pearson, com-
from San Francisco, with 184 pas-
90 dollars to E. Flint, agent, P. M

hip Northerner, H. Randall, com-
from San Francisco, with 181 pas-
£811, dollars to E. Flint, Agent, P

le, F. David Captain, 23 days from
and passengers to Captain.
Jose Gonzales, 6 days from Man-
k to M. M. Anderson
trvis, R. Joy, Commander 10 days
6 passenger, and 666.475 dollars
to the agent of the company.
intertir, 8 Sisbana, Captain, 82
on, with provisions to Serrays &

Comberd. Captain 22 days from
and general cargo to M. Arrivet
ar, Diguine. 18 from E. G. Fan-
31 days from San Diaz, with &C.

lather Francis, Capt. Coggins. 12
, assorted cargo to H. G. Ry.

TARY CARD.

BOARD SHIP RUSSELL,
OGA, MARCH, 21, 1852.
unfavorable to the condi-
ell, and censuring LUIS
ner, (unjustly as the un-
er a full examination of
s and number of passen-

therefore, that the ship
 condition as represented

a the opinion of the un-
n, Esq., owner of said

PANAMA RAILROAD,
For ASPINWALL, (Navy Bay.)

A TRAIN OF CARS

WILL leave "*BOHIO SOLDADO*"
DAILY, on and after Monday, March 15,
at 4 o'clock, P. M. Passengers leaving Gorgona in the morning, will reach Aspinwall
the same day. The United States Steamers
will, in future, come into Navy Bay, to land
and receive Passengers, the U. S. Mails and
Specie.

Passengers will land and embark at Aspinwall from the Company's Wharf *free of charge*
Fare on the Railroad from *Bohio Soldado* to
to *Aspinwall* is fixed at the low rate of $2
(*Two Dollars.*)

Passengers from the United States leave
Aspinwall at half past six o'clock, A. M., and
arrive at Gorgona same day.

For further information inquire at the Rail-
road Office in Gorgona.
CHARLES H. GREEN, *Agent.*
Aspinwall, March 12, 1852. [mar23-1m

The "*Echo*," "*Star*," and "*El Panameño,*"
of this city; and the "*Herald*" and "*Alta,*"
of San Francisco, will please publish the above
one month, and send bills to this office.

United States Mail Steamship Company.

NOTICE TO THE

OFFICE OF THE SHIP
LADY GOUGH,
FOR SAN FRANCISCO,
Main Street, **opposite the Orleans
House.**
mar12-tf   CAMPBELL, JONES & CO.

For *SAN FRANCISCO--Direct.*

THE A1 coppered and copper-fas-
tened ship

LADY GOUGH,

1500 *Tons Burthen,*

To sail on or about
FRIDAY, MARCH 26TH.

This vessel is well ventilated, and wil lnot
carry more passengers than allowed by law.
The between decks run from stem to stern
and the demensions are 150 feet long by 31 feet
broad.

The Provisions will be of the best quality,
and Water will be supplied liberally.
Apply to   CAMPBELL, JONES & CO.
mar12   Opposite the Orleans House.

FOR SAN FRANCISCO--Direct.

THE New Splendid Clipper A1
American Packet Ship
VALPARAISO,

2000 *Tons Burthen,*

Captain G. W. KELHAM, will have
IMMEDIATE DESPATCH
for the above Port.

(right margin fragments)

Will

S

Si
affo
Cali
diou
m

N.

TO

T

2,1

Ha
ulti
abo
vid
wil

?
two
she
the

and New Granada—a signal for cheers—cheers for the new city of Aspinwall, cheers for President Stephens, cheers for Mr. Law, and cheers for New Granada.

DIFFICULTIES MOUNT HIGH

Activity continued to accelerate in Aspinwall, and railroad line progress became more evident. Hotels and warehouses were built, and large docks were constructed to accommodate ships of twenty-foot draft. Some vessels discharged at docks and others at anchor. Trainloads of rock and earth were constantly on their way to be dumped from trestles where the railroad crossed the lowlands.

Work was pushed until the railroad was completed to Bohío Soldado—a section of track that passed through Black Swamp in a 3,000-foot stretch of "silt and water"[20] between Lion Hill and Ahorca Lagarto, where Colonel Totten could not find bottom at 180 feet. It was at this critical time, in a notice signed March 12, 1852, and effective March 15, that the Panama Railroad Company published its first train schedule in the *Panama Herald* March 23, announcing daily train departures from Bohío Soldado to Aspinwall, fare to be $2.00 per passenger.

The road was then sixteen miles from Aspinwall, with thirty-one miles left to complete. The passengers, after leaving the train, still had to pole their way in native bungos to Gorgona or Cruces before shifting to the final lap of discomfort on pack mules to Panamá. At Bohío Soldado a sandstone quarry was established. Although the rock was soft, it was sound and quarryable in large sizes. Used in abutments, piers, drains, and wharves, there was no evidence of deterioration after twenty years of service.[21]

Another section was opened to Frijoles about May 1, but the rainy season was setting in again and, as usual in Panamá, outdoor work slowed down. Even so, by the end of the month it

[20] *Canal Record*, July 29, 1908, I, 377 (U.S.).
[21] *Panama Star and Herald*, Sept. 4, 1879.

was announced that trains would leave Tavernilla—still further reducing river travel. The company planned to carry on to Barbacoas, a place named after the Indian word for "bridge." There the railroad would cross the Chagres. From that point it was decided to complete the railroad by contract with M. C. Story, who was to start by building the Barbacoas bridge and to complete the road in one year.

In July the company advertised that trains would leave for Aspinwall from Barbacoas daily. With twenty-three and one-quarter miles constructed and twenty-five still unfinished, so strong was the desire to eliminate the boat trip on the Chagres that there were great hopes of completing the bridge and running trains to Gorgona by September.

Hardly had train service been extended to Barbacoas when the railroad received its first military test by the United States. On July 16, 1852, eight companies of the Fourth Infantry, United States Army, numbering about 700, including the families, together with some 300 passengers additional, arrived at Aspinwall on the United States mail steamer "Ohio," en route to California for garrison duty. Landing too late for that day's one train, the regiment remained in Aspinwall overnight at a time when the rainy season had set in, flooding the streets, and when cholera was epidemic on the Isthmus. By the next morning most of the baggage had been loaded on cars, but the locomotive proved too light to carry more than half the troops, and two trains had to be dispatched at one-hour intervals, baggage being left for a later trip.

Arriving at Barbacoas, where the railroad's facilities for transit to Panamá City ended, the regiment was divided, the main body going to Gorgona by the slow method of pole-propelled boats and thence marching to Panamá. One company under the regimental quartermaster, Captain U. S. Grant, with the sick, the women and children, and the baggage, was ordered to Cruces, a few miles beyond Gorgona. There mule transportation to Panamá was supposed to be ready, under the terms of a previous army contract by which the steamship company assumed the entire cost and responsibility for the regiment's transportation to California by both land and water, acting through its agents along the route. But the company's local agent could not obtain mules for the troops because of higher prices paid by the civilian passengers. Grant waited three days; then he himself hired mules at double the agent's price, charging it to the shipping company, and resumed the journey to Panamá.

Because of this delay and the exposure to rains at Cruces and the inability of the Gorgona troops to make headway in the mud the transit was not executed as planned. Cholera and jungle fever attacked the troops along both routes, so depleting the small guard at Cruces that baggage had to go unprotected, subject to native thievery and to local infection that later compelled some of it to be destroyed. In addition, the troops ate contaminated local fruits and drank indiscriminately along the way, thus adding to the sickness. Order or organization en route became impossible and the movement developed into a straggle, each one for himself. The troops arrived at Panamá wet and muddy, tired and hungry. Some arrived drunk, some sick, and some did not arrive at all, having died in the mud along the way.

When the regiment, after four weeks' delay on the Isthmus, finally reached California late in August, about eighty of the men had died, besides nearly as many of their women and children. The experiences encountered on the Isthmus have been told by the regimental surgeon,[22] who lived constantly in vital and responsible contact with the officers, the men, and their families.

As a result of these unfortunate delays, Captain Grant, later to become General of the Armies and President, obtained some very unfavorable local editorial publicity—interesting in the light of his subsequent distinguished career. The comment

[22] Dr. C. S. Tripler, *Report of the Regimental Surgeon, Fourth Infantry, to Surgeon General, Sept. 14, 1852*, pp. 454–58 (U.S.). A. D. Richardson, *Personal History of Ulysses S. Grant,* chapter 10.

states: "Unfitted by either natural ability or education for the post he occupied, he evinced his incapacity at every moment."[23]

Captain Grant's experiences on the Isthmus must have impressed him deeply, for early in his first term as President of the United States he secured from Colombia and from the United States Congress the authority which enabled the United States Navy to conduct the first comprehensive survey of Isthmian canal routes, 1870–1875.

On the part of the railroad, little time was lost in starting the bridge across the Chagres at Barbacoas, where the river was about 300 feet wide and subject to great changes during the heavy rains, becoming then a destructive torrent. When the bridge was nearly completed, a sudden freshet of the raging Chagres swept away one span—an accident which prevented continuation of the railroad to Gorgona during the dry season of 1852.

Another great loss came to the company in the passing of its president, John L. Stephens, who had been the dominating genius in the enterprise. After having been exposed to great hardships and diseases he returned to New York, where he died October 13, 1852, from a malady contracted on the Isthmus. He was succeeded by William C. Young.

The collapse of the bridge, the death of President Stephens, the illness and death of many workmen—all added to the difficulties of the company, and work bogged down. Although the railroad was supposed to be completed by the contractor in October 1853, not only was the Barbacoas bridge still unfinished but only about a tenth of the contract work had been accomplished.

The Isthmians lamented the lack of the railway, they lamented the lack of activity, and they regretted the setting in of the wet season with so little being done except surveys by the engineers, " 'ho perform mysterious evolutions . . . . looking through complicated instruments at long staffs, driving stakes

[23] *Panama Herald,* Aug. 17, 1852.

into the ground, rushing about woods and . . . . swamps in all
directions . . . . and then disappearing as secretly as they arrived." There were no "stalwart laborers" clearing the soil or
making the forest ring with the "stroke of the axe." The Isthmians thought that thousands of workers should have been engaged in constructing the railroad. Instead, the line was still
the "birthplace of tropical vegetation and the haunt of the beast
of prey."[24]

Complaints from passengers about the loss of baggage also
received public notice. The inefficiency, the risk, and the uncertainty of the baggage service combined to cause discontent
among the riding public and often forced passengers to wait in
Panamá for delivery of their valuables and to miss their ships,
or to sail, leaving valuables behind. With rates for passengers
from Cruces to Panamá by mule at $18 per person and 17 cents
per pound for baggage, it is not strange that complaints concerning the poor service were so numerous.

Again a reorganization occurred. The contractor, unable to
handle his contract within the price limit, was relieved and the
work taken over by the company. President Young resigned
and was succeeded by David Hoadley.

A NEW LEADERSHIP

Among the first activities under the new leadership was the
recruiting of more labor. Men came from all over the world—
Ireland, Hindustan, China, England, France, Germany, and
Austria—in all, more than 7,000 men. Selected because they
were able-bodied, many of the workers did not thrive in Panamá
because of the vast difference in climatic conditions. The company tried hard to meet their special needs, even going so far
in the case of the 1,000 Chinese as to provide them with "hill-
rice, their tea, and opium."[25] But so unhappy were the Chinese
that many committed suicide—a fact which gave rise to the

[24] *Panama Herald*, March 11, 1853.
[25] F. N. Otis, *Isthmus of Panama*, p. 35.

curious fable that Matachin was so named to commemorate dead Chinese, since in Spanish *mata* means kill and *Chino* means Chinese. As a matter of historical interest, Matachin is shown on maps of this region published as early as 1678.[26]

Disease became so rampant and desertions so common among the workers that it was necessary to import large numbers of Jamaicans as replacements, and construction was on again.

Reconstruction was started on a new Barbacoas bridge across the Chagres, to be 625 feet long and 18 feet wide, to be made with wrought-iron girders, and to stand 40 feet above the water. It was to be one of the "longest and finest iron bridges in the world." Actually the bridge was rebuilt so strong that it lasted more than half a century and was used by the railroad even after the United States occupied the Canal Zone. The iron girders, supported by rock masonry piers and abutments quarried at San Pablo, gave the appearance of strength and durability, while the American pine in the bridge, imported from Darien, Georgia,[27] suggested a linking of the oceans. Along the rest of the road many temporary bridge structures were replaced with permanent culverts or bridges, using "masonry abutments, and iron superstructures." Original soft-wood crossties were replaced with lignum vitae ties, which were so hard that holes had to be bored before spikes were driven and so durable that when sections of track were taken up in 1910 the ties were still unrotted.

From Panamá, construction became active, pushing toward the Atlantic. In June 1853, the railroad company erected buildings near the north city gate on the Playa Prieta for use of workmen and started clearing the right of way at Panamá. It was rumored that the company had bought Flamenco, Perico, and Naos Islands. It should be remembered that access to deep water at Panamá City was long the primary aim of those engaged in shipping, as the large tidal range on the Pacific caused vessels to ground at low tide in the harbors.

[26] G. W. Davis, article quoted in *Canal Record* (Dec. 25, 1907), I, 133 (U.S.).
[27] Robert Tomes, *Panama in 1855*, p. 82.

In August, conditions once more looked promising. Colonel Totten, the experienced chief engineer, took charge again after failure of the contractor and pushed work with his characteristic force and determination. Gleefully it was announced that contractor Story had been pushed overboard and that the increase in activity had had a "magical effect"; the faces of the merchants "shortened and their purse strings . . . . loosened," many betting that the road would be completed within ten months—the completion, of course, being the omen for a "glorious future."[28]

Progress everywhere was reported, hills were leveled, and ravines were filled with the spoil as preparation of the right of way continued. It was expected that the railroad would be completed all the way by August of the next year. "Where would the Nicaragua transit be then?" asked the elated Isthmians. But in spite of their wishful thinking, nothing had been done to repair the muddy Cruces road so that transit from Aspinwall could be made in one day. The transit continued to be an arduous undertaking in spite of the screams of locomotive whistles frequently heard in Panamá. Even in early September, passengers required thirty-six hours to cross the Isthmus!

But events were developing rapidly to speed up Isthmian transit. The Barbacoas bridge was nearing completion. The Cruces road, long a difficult and muddy trail, was being repaired by young Ran Runnels, former Texas ranger, and in September a mail transit of twelve hours was made while the railroad was being pushed with the work of 1,000 men.

Trains had been running for about two years when, on October 1, 1853, the 3:30 P.M. train pulled out of Aspinwall with 600 passengers. Passing the Monkey Hill Station, it slowly approached Tavernilla, where a sharp curve in a cut contained a bridge, the view of which was obscured. A bull was sighted on the bridge, but the train was too close to stop before colliding with the beast in what was the first fatal accident on the Panama Railroad. The locomotive, four baggage cars, and two crowded

[28] *Panama Star*, Aug. 21, 1853.

passenger cars plunged into the valley, killing two—a native and a North American on his way to California. But this accident did not delay the railroad work.[29]

Accidents were not the only difficulty to distract Colonel Totten. Repair of the Cruces road was nearing completion, with workers paid at the rate of 80 cents per day. To stimulate efforts and to reduce turnover among employees, Colonel Totten authorized a bonus of an additional 40 cents a day to all workmen who remained until the work was completed. This satisfied the men at first, but the local judge at Cruces saw a financial opportunity for himself. He told the workers, 150 strong, that if each of them would pay him a dollar he would require their superintendent to pay the full $1.20 a day, regardless of whether they remained with the railroad or not—a proposition readily accepted. The judge, accompanied by a group of soldiers, then arrested the superintendent, placed him in irons like a criminal, and dragged him through the streets to the prison, where he was told he would not be released except on payment of some money. After a few days, friends interceded and obtained release but not redress. The only result of the entire episode was to delay the work of completing the Cruces road.[30] Even with the repair work already done, it still required seven to eight hours to reach Cruces from Panamá.

COMPLETION OF THE RAILROAD

In November 1853, Colonel Totten could clearly foresee the future problems involved in completion of the railroad. To prepare for the approaching dry season he reported the conditions to the directors. Over seven miles of grading from Chagres River to the Obispo was nearly finished, with about three miles of track laid. He expected the Barbacoas bridge to be completed by December 1, and that would have permitted the running of trains to Gorgona and to the Obispo River by the next January 1. With the Cruces road repaired and with the completion of a branch road extending from it to the Obispo, it was planned to transfer passengers and freight directly from the steam train to the pack mules when the trains reached the latter place. This connection would have enabled transit in twelve hours without a boat ride.

Grading and clearing the right of way along the Obispo and at Panamá had already started. Of the 48 miles in total length of road, about 23 were in operation to Barbacoas and it was expected that 30 miles would be in operation by January 1, so that only 18 would remain to be completed. It was in this remaining portion, Colonel Totten stated, that the summit ridge had to be crossed at an elevation of 250 feet above Pacific high tide. He considered the ground favorable, with the largest cut at the summit 1,300 feet long by 24 feet deep and the total excavation about 30,000 cubic yards. On the basis of performance by Mr. Story, he estimated that with 4,570 men the road could be completed to the Pacific within six months—that is, by August 1854. But he was hesitant in giving an exact prediction, for he had had too much experience in the Isthmian area to venture definite forecasts. He did point out, however, that all materials had to be imported, even timber for ties, which were obtained from either the United States or New Granada. As for workers, they also had to be imported, at a cost per worker varying from $15 to $50. As to sickness, although it was an important item, he emphasized its exaggeration by showing that it was actually less than the average of public-works projects in our Western States. Iron for the entire railroad was on the Isthmus, and the remaining expenditure to complete the railroad was estimated at $1,426,800.[31]

The Panama Railroad at this time had eight locomotives, twelve first-class cars, 100 platform cars, and 100 dirt cars, one foundry, one carpenter shop, and one blacksmith shop; the entire road was employing 1,400 men and had main offices and repair shops located at Aspinwall. It is no wonder that Colonel

[31] *Ibid.*, Dec. 22, 1853.

Totten proudly considered his railroad "as perfect a road as can be found in the United States." He felt secure, with iron for the rest of the railroad on the Isthmus ready for use. The entire railroad force had grown to 2,500, with 1,200 on the Obispo section.

But already visitors to hotels had begun to complain of the noise so suggestive of present-day life on the Isthmus. After a visit to Aspinwall one writer wrote that "the 'snorting of the iron horse' as it coursed up and down the railroad in front of the Hotel"[32] had awakened him early.

On November 24, 1853, another milepost was passed in the history of the railroad. One witness of the event wrote: "The Rubicon is passed. The great obstacle is overthrown. This day at 11 o'clock A.M. precisely, the pilot train passed over the great bridge at Barbacoas with flying colors. There were one locomotive and nine cars, heavily laden with freight and passengers."[33] Of course there was a celebration!

Nicaragua, the ancient Panamá competitor for interocean traffic, was at this time also very active as a highway of travel. To offset the competition the press announced that after January 1, 1854, trains would run from Obispo to Aspinwall, that the road from Obispo to Cruces was open, and that a trip between the two oceans could be made in eight hours. Appealing to the prospective traveler for confidence and imploring him not to credit false rumors, the announcement concluded: "As to all the nonsense about malaria, fever, pestilential swamps and the thousand other ills that are charged to the Isthmus, we repeat again, they exist no more than in any other tropical climate, and that prudence and ordinary precaution is all that is required on the part of unacclimated passengers."[34]

In January 1854 the working forces were augmented by the arrival of 360 Irish railroad laborers—all young men about twenty years old, healthy and able-bodied, but not so efficient on

[32] *Panama Star*, Nov. 8, 1853.
[33] *Ibid.*, Nov. 30, 1853.   [34] *Ibid.*, Dec. 24, 1853.

the Isthmus as in the cooler climates. Even so, Colonel Totten estimated that they would do a fair amount of work during the first four or six months. The next month about 3,000 workers were engaged on the eighteen miles between Obispo and Panamá, presenting the energetic activity which so often has appeared to Latin Americans as the chief characteristic of the Anglo-Saxon race. To Colonel Totten this activity gave rise to the hope that the rails would join the oceans in August, and the progress was shown by changing the daily advertisement in the Panamá papers as each completed section advanced toward the Pacific. On February 14 it was advertised that trains ran daily from Aspinwall to Obispo, leaving Aspinwall at 9 A.M. and reaching Obispo at 2 P.M. Fare was $12.50 one way for one passenger and 100 pounds of baggage.

The young Irishmen from Cork proved better than expected and were reported becoming more useful daily and enjoying "generally excellent health," as the work on the railroad was being pushed toward the summit and while Panamá was waiting anxiously to have the "iron horse snorting"[35] near by. On March 30 came the announcement for the particular benefit of the California public that transit time was now six hours, and on July 13 trains ran to within one mile of Summit—only eleven and one-half miles from Panamá.

One day near Summit a wounded Irishman, John McGlynn, was attacked, robbed, and left to die. He was discovered by the former Texas ranger, Ran Runnels. With the local government impotent to enforce law and order in this area, which so often had been subjected to unrestricted robbery and murder of travelers, it was necessary to take prompt measures. Ran Runnels offered to organize a mounted guard of twenty men to clear the Isthmus of murderers and robbers, and it was published that foreigners would be protected whether the impotent local government liked it or not.[36] Runnels was vested with complete authority by the

[35] *Ibid.*, March 29, 1854.
[36] *Panama Star and Herald*, July 18, 1854.

railroad and the government. He proceeded to hunt down the murderers and robbers, using the very efficacious method of "whipping, imprisonment, and shooting down in emergency."[37] It was not long before there was a "regular stampede among the undesirables" to leave the Isthmus without saying goodbye.

When the government no longer feared its incapacity, after the expulsion of the criminals, the authority of Ran Runnels was revoked, although the excellent quality of his work was greatly appreciated. The protection of the railroad then returned to the feeble hands of the New Granadan Government.

Late in September the railroad was completed to Summit, and of the remaining part to Panamá only four miles of grading and seven miles of rail were uncompleted. For some time in 1854 the terminus was at Culebra, a little native village beyond Empire. There sprang up a thriving village which boasted of its hotels that had been "imported ready-made from the United States, into which often more than a thousand men, women, and children were promiscuously stowed"[38] for a night stopover on the transit trip. As the completed section of the railroad advanced, the terminus shifted southward with its activities. Construction gangs worked from both ends to hasten the day of joining the rails. On October 28 another advance was marked when the Panama Railroad advertised train schedules from Aspinwall to Summit.

Colonel Totten then estimated the railroad would be completed in January, and he wanted to make a ceremony of the event. On November 15, 1854, he wrote to one of the directors, Gouverneur Kemble, suggesting that as many directors as possible attend the celebration and look over the work. He alluded to the "difficulties overcome" but which did not impress him. Not boasting, he expressed quite opposite feelings: "I am ashamed that so much has been expended in overcoming so little, and take no credit for any engineering science displayed on the work. The difficulties have been of another nature,

---

[37] Tomes, *op. cit.*, p. 124.   [38] Otis, *op. cit.*, p. 121.

and do not show themselves on the line."[39] Perhaps he was too modest in this statement, for it was his determination that pushed construction to completion, and his achievement is recognized today by a suitable memorial plate in the Panama Railroad Station at Panamá City.

Conversation in Panamá next centered around the plans for the inauguration. Some wanted a parade, some a dinner, and others a ball. But the *Star and Herald* characterized a parade as a funeral, feared a dinner would be dry, and did not like a ball because it had another plan. It was for a picnic trip by the railroad to the bank of the Chagres: "A trip to the Chagres and back, a breakfast, dance and lunch on its banks, all in one day: why, such a thing was never heard of before, and the mention of it would have been laughed at as ridiculous five years ago."[40]

At last on January 27, 1855, rail-laying gangs were in sight of each other, and at midnight at Summit in "darkness and rain, the last rail was laid,"[41] at a point thirty-seven miles from Aspinwall and ten and a half from Panamá. The next day was Sunday. Large crowds gathered along the line to see the first trans-Isthmian train. Warning of its approach by the shrill sound of the whistle, it came "thundering over the summit, and down the Pacific slope" as a "chariot of fire" on what to them was a "perilous journey, over fearful chasms, through mountain gorges, along pleasant valleys, winding around hoary mountain tops, perched upon a narrow shelf of rock in mid-air."[42] It had also passed through jungle and forest and crossed swamps and rivers as it carried distinguished guests, headed by Colonel Totten and Vice-President Alexander J. Center, on the historic ride.

As the "iron horse" rattled along cautiously into Panamá, the people, impressed by the appearance of the train and the "facility with which the wild creature was handled,"[43] gave hearty cheers. They felt that at last the great panacea for all

---

[39] *Panama Star and Herald*, Dec. 19, 1854.   [40] *Ibid.*, Jan. 23, 1855.
[41] Otis, *op. cit.*, p. 36.   [42] *Aspinwall Daily Courier*, Feb. 24, 1855.
[43] *Panama Star and Herald*, Jan. 30, 1855.

their troubles had come. They saw the end of mules and saddles as well as the muddy and difficult Cruces road, with a capacious railroad car as a welcome substitute. They hailed the "Yankee enterprise" which in five years had completed what the British and French had been unable to carry through.

It was not long before the Isthmians realized that the millennium was not at hand. Those who formerly had been in the pack-mule business were thrown out of work. Business did not increase overnight to offset the effect of the losses. To this disappointment was added the dissatisfaction with trans-Isthmian rates, which were advertised as $25 each way, although monthly commutation tickets for $50 were allowed to residents.

Why this railroad had such high rates is not clear. The Superintendent, Colonel Center, said that they "were intended to be, to a certain extent, prohibitory, until we could get things in shape,"[44] after which it was apparently his idea to reduce rates. But the high rates were retained for many years, during which the road established its great reputation as a dividend payer.

Finally the time of formal celebration arrived, as the distinguished guests collected at Panamá. It began with the arrival of the dignitaries on the steamer "George Law" at Aspinwall on February 15, 1855, with almost five hundred passengers on the way to California but just in time to join the celebration.

The next morning, as their train proceeded, there were demonstrations along the line, made effective by inscribed floral arches over the road. Upon reaching Matachin the train stopped. The crowd alighted and went to a nearby hill to dedicate a monument amid a deluge of perfervid oratory.[45] The journey was just as quickly resumed to Panamá. The gold seekers sailed for the West without delay, but the program for the celebrants was only started.

----

[44] Tracy Robinson, *Panama: A Personal Record of Forty-six Years, 1861–1907*, p. 24.

[45] *Aspinwall Daily Courier*, Feb. 24, 1855.

On the following day, Saturday morning, February 17, 1855, directors and stockholders, steamship agents, and guests embarked on the "Columbus" for a trip to Taboga Island. Landing amid the roar of guns from all the ships in the harbor, they were entertained at lunch by Captain Wild of the British ship "Bolivia," with the "substantiality and cordiality of a good old English welcome."[46] Then there was a visit to the steamer "John L. Stephens," which had gone around the Horn, and for an interlude in the afternoon there came a tropical shower and a good drenching for many. In the evening Colonel Totten entertained eighty guests at dinner at Aspinwall House. Toasts were made to the President of the United States, to the Governor of Panamá, to the President of the Panama Railroad, to the press, and to the agents of the shipping companies at Panamá. On the following Tuesday the exhausted guests returned to Aspinwall to embark for New York, and the railroad people returned to normal. The period of construction was over, and the Isthmus gradually slumped back into its monotonous existence.

The road as completed in 1855 was about forty-seven and a half miles long. Starting at Aspinwall on Manzanillo Island, the road followed Limon Bay, crossed the Mindi River, and reached the Chagres at Gatun. Then, following the valley of the Chagres, it crossed the river at Barbacoas and continued along the Chagres to the Obispo River, the valley of which it followed on its way to Summit. After passing the summit of the Isthmian cordillera the road descended along the valley of the Rio Grande to Panamá City. The total length of the railroad was 47 miles and 3,020 feet. The total cost of the railroad until completion of the construction in 1859 was about $8,000,000.

Loss of life among construction laborers was not large, except in the case of the Chinese. They resisted medical treatment, exposed themselves to bad weather, used opium, became panic-stricken, and committed suicide. Out of a total force estimated by Colonel Totten to have been about 6,000, deaths numbered

[46] *Panama Star and Herald*, Feb. 20, 1855.

835 (whites 295, blacks 140, and Chinese 400). In constructing the road, about 140,000 ties were used.[47] When the number
of ties used is compared with the actual number of deaths, we
have facts which throw into irrefutable discard the widely quoted
and alluring fable of a "dead man for every tie."

Furthermore, it was demonstrated quite effectively that the
Isthmus possessed no important resources in labor, capital, material, food, or clothing, but required importation of all these
essentials. From the United States came the leaders—the "capitalists, the men of science, the engineers, the practical business
managers, the superior workmen, the masons, carpenters, and
forgers of iron."[48] Ireland, Jamaica, India, China, and Colombia supplied the bulk of the labor. Even Colonel Totten himself
said the Isthmus afforded nothing which could be used in the
construction of the railroad, necessitating the importation of
all materials, even crossties, which had to be brought from
Cartagena or from the United States. Was this condition prophetic of future difficulties when the time for greater construction projects should arrive?

The completion of the railroad across the Isthmus was for
many the realization of an age-old dream. For the promoters
it was the launching of a singularly profitable business enterprise. For those with greater vision, to have an operating railroad practically running along the line of the future canal,
ready for use when the day of canal construction should come,
was an essential prerequisite for digging any canal. The railroad stimulated United States commerce and hastened the settlement of the West. It gave to Panamá a tremendous advantage
in the choice of a route for the first canal. It educated engineers
in the geography of the Isthmus and interested them in the problems of an Isthmian canal. It was the first step in constructing
a waterway, forever placing the builders of the Panama Railroad as the real pioneers of the Panama Canal.

[47] G. W. Davis, article quoted in *Canal Record* (Dec. 25, 1907), I, 133.
[48] Tomes, *Panama in 1855*, p. 112.

Panama Railroad Bridge over the Chagres at Barbacoas
From F. N. Otis, *Illustrated History of the Panama Railroad*, 1861

FERDINAND DE LESSEPS, 1805–1894
From statue in the Plaza de Francia, Panama City

CHAPTER II

FROM SUEZ TO PANAMA

I have never been alarmed by the obstacles thrown in the path of a great enterprise, nor by the delays which discussion and contradictory arguments entail, my experience having taught me that what is accomplished too quickly has no deep roots.—FERDINAND DE LESSEPS, builder of the Suez Canal.[1]

PRELUDE TO THE PARIS CONGRESS

While Colonel Totten was completing the railroad across the Isthmus of Panamá, another man, inspired by the efforts of Egyptian rulers for over 3,000 years, was starting a great project destined to realize the dream of the Pharaohs. Overcoming incredible difficulties, hardships, and determined opposition by the rivals of France, he succeeded in opening the Suez Canal to the commerce of the world on November 17, 1869, obtaining such rare distinction in the eyes of the French nation that he was universally acclaimed as "The Great Frenchman." That man was Ferdinand de Lesseps.

But he did not rest. In the following years he began to think of the Isthmus of Panamá, which he studied seriously. Then came the devastating defeat of France in the Franco-Prussian War, 1870–71. This in turn was followed by the natural desire of the French nation to offset its defeat by a great project of peace as the first step in revival of its position of power and prestige. The Panama Canal was a great concept that would rank with Suez. When the name of De Lesseps was associated with Panamá, the idea of the Panama Canal attained universal appeal.

The concept of a canal at Panamá was posed in 1871 at the International Geographical Congress at Antwerp, as a result of many explorations in Colombia by Anthoine de Gogorza, who was born in the United States of French parents and had lived

[1] De Lesseps, *Recollections of Forty Years*, II, 202.

31

for years in Colombia. But it was not until 1875, when De Lesseps was presiding over the Geographical Society of Paris, that
the subject received wide public attention. Until then De Lesseps had preferred the project of a lock canal at Nicaragua but
had to give up the idea because of the predominant interest of
the United States in that field. He had experienced the tremendous success of his sea-level canal at Suez, which was paying
dividends to small shareholders rather than to powerful financiers. Because of its success the canal at Suez became to the
French people the idealized type, and therefore they called for
a sea-level canal at Panamá.

At this 1875 meeting there was insufficient knowledge to
permit detailed discussions; but De Lesseps, reflecting the trend
of the times, claimed a sea-level canal was the only one capable
of meeting the needs of navigation and that failure of the early
planners to examine the matter of a sea-level route, as well as a
lock-canal route, was a great error. The result was a resolution
calling for an international congress to collect evidence and
evaluate all information and then to make definite recommendations for a canal. A Committee of Initiative, with De Lesseps
at its head, was formed and made efforts toward securing international co-operation in conducting surveys. De Gogorza was
sent back to Colombia.

Meanwhile the efforts of the United States to secure canal
rights, which had been interrupted by the Civil War, were
resumed under President Johnson; but the treaty signed with
Colombia in January 1869 was rejected by the Colombian Senate. The succeeding administration of President Grant continued negotiations, and a treaty was signed on January 26, 1870;
but this was so amended by the Colombian Senate as to make
it unacceptable to the United States Government. Because of
the undeveloped means of communication of that day and the
consequent delay of messages, further canal negotiations were
transferred in 1873 from Bogotá to Washington, where they likewise failed.

During this period the explorations and surveys authorized by Congress in the early part of Grant's first term had been progressing over the various routes—Darien, Tehuantepec, Nicaragua, and Panamá, 1870–1875—with a thoroughness and precision unequaled by previous explorers and civil engineers. In March 1872, Congress authorized the President to appoint an Interoceanic Canal Commission to study and evaluate the reports of these surveys and other reliable material, with a view to determining the most practicable route for a waterway between the two oceans. In February 1876 the Commission made its report, recommending the Nicaragua route. Any further attempts by the United States to renew negotiations with Colombia were thus rendered useless, and attention was directed toward Nicaragua.[2]

Moreover, the United States Congress, under pressure for strict economy in the country-wide period of drought and depression, by its Appropriations Act of August 13, 1876, cut out all provisions for the legations in Bolivia, Colombia, and Ecuador, in addition to many in Europe. Grant, under protest, was thus forced to withdraw the ministers and close these legations for the rest of his term.[3]

Fortunately for the French, these events left the way open for De Gogorza to work unopposed in Bogotá. He convinced the Colombian Government that he knew a practicable route in the San Blas region where the Atrato and Tuyra rivers could be utilized, and on May 28, 1876, obtained a contract which required a report on explorations within eighteen months. He then returned to France.

In Paris the Geographical Society had organized the Committee of Initiative to examine the subject of an interoceanic canal, with De Lesseps as its president and with Admiral Baron

[2] S. F. Bemis, *The American Secretaries of State and Their Diplomacy*, VII, 206–9. Allan Nevins, *Hamilton Fish: The Inner History of the Grant Administration*, Appendix I, pp. 913–15.

[3] State Dept., *Register, 1876–1878* (U.S.). *New York Tribune*, Aug. 16, 1876, p. 1; Aug. 12, p. 1.

de la Roncière-le Noury, president of the Georgraphical Society, and J. L. J. Meurand, Director of Consulates in the Paris Foreign Office, as vice-presidents. But geographical knowledge of the Isthmus was insufficient, and to obtain more information it was necessary to finance additional explorations and surveys. Accordingly, a limited company, La Société Civile Internationale du Canal Interocéanique, was organized by General Istvan Türr, aide-de-camp to the King of Italy; Lucien N. B. Wyse, a lieutenant in the French Navy and a grandson of Lucien Bonaparte; and shrewd Baron Jacques de Reinach, naturalized Frenchman and financier. It was a real "combination of geography and finance," and the society took over the Colombian concession of De Gogorza.

Wyse, a dominant influence in the formation of the society, was authorized to explore the Isthmus. Selecting Armand Réclus, a naval lieutenant, as his chief assistant, he sailed for Panamá; but three of his eight engineers died on the way.

Wyse divided his expedition into groups and explored several routes in the Darien-Atrato regions. Completing his work in April 1877, he returned to Paris with plans which De Lesseps promptly rejected because all required tunnels and locks. So Wyse had to visit the Isthmus again and was able to start his second exploration on December 6, 1877, this time in Panamá. There he examined two routes, the San Blas and the present canal route from Limon Bay to Panamá, and chose the latter. His plan was a sea-level project, conveniently near the railroad and with a 7,720-meter tunnel through Culebra.

Armed with this sea-level plan for the Panama Canal, he left for Bogotá, a trip that required him to spend eleven days on horseback. It was in this isolated South American capital that, in the name of his society, he negotiated what is known as the Wyse Concession and signed it with the Minister of Foreign Affairs, Eustorgio Salgar, on March 20, 1878. That day marks the legal start of the Panama Canal.

Wyse returned to France via New York, where he made arrangements for securing control of the Panama Railroad. He landed in France not only with his reports of explorations and a concession from Colombia but with assurance of control of the railroad that was required as an adjunct to French construction. With the reports of Wyse available for De Lesseps, together with those of the extensive explorations during Grant's Administration as evaluated by the United States Interoceanic Canal Commission in its report of February 1876, the great canal promoter was in a position to proceed with the next step.

De Lesseps had learned many lessons at Suez. Besides, he was an experienced diplomat, acquainted with the ways of the world. He knew the need for that nebulous thing called international co-operation in the launching of great projects in foreign lands and counted upon this to quiet foreign opposition, the nature of which he fully understood. He did not like engineers; he had had to resolve too many disputes between them at Suez.

Invitations were sent out by the Geographical Society of Paris to "all the savants, engineers, and sailors of the Old and New World,"[4] as well as to chambers of commerce and geographical societies, asking each to send delegates for an international congress to meet in Paris on May 15, 1879.

What were the forces behind all this movement? There were disinterested geographers and also shrewd financiers who owned the concession and who desired to sell their holdings; but these men could not be expected to leave Paris for the frontier life at Panamá. Furthermore, there were many—leaders, engineers, and explorers—who, inspired by the vision of the French nation as the creator of the other great waterway of the world, were willing to follow their calling to the jungles of Panamá. There was De Lesseps!

THE PARIS CONGRESS

The International Congress for Consideration of an Interoceanic Canal (Congrès International d'Études du Canal Inter-

---

[4] De Lesseps, *op. cit.*, II, 176.

océanique) met at Paris on May 15, 1879, under the temporary chairmanship of Admiral Baron de la Roncière-le Noury, with a total of 135 delegates. Its members were celebrated in the fields of "science, politics, and industry." Seventy-four were from France. The eleven from the United States included men interested in Nicaragua and other canal areas. Ferdinand de Lesseps was chosen for the presidency, which he assumed with all his characteristic force, enthusiasm, and confidence. Admiral Daniel Ammen[5] was made first vice-president and sat on De Lesseps' right.

The Congress was organized in five committees. There was the Statistical Commission, with M. Pierre E. Levasseur presiding, whose task was to determine whether the probable tonnage passing through the canal would be sufficient to provide expected returns on invested capital. It predicted that 5,250,000 tons would be the normal traffic, that it would be developed gradually after the assumed opening in 1889, and that 2,000,000 tons would be diverted from the trade then existing between Europe and Asia.[6] But it would be possible to handle an annual traffic of even 6,000,000 tons, the Secretary-General of the Suez Canal advised, provided fifty ships could be transited in a day. That, De Lesseps said, was the reason that the Suez was a sealevel and not a lock canal—a view which produced its effect on the members.

Nathan Appleton, of Boston, headed the Economic Commission. It reported on distances to be saved by use of the Panama Canal, the new markets to be opened and new traffic created, and the reductions on freight and insurance to be effected by the shortening of voyages and the avoidance of dangerous areas like Cape Horn. This Commission also mentioned the adverse effects of locks or tunnels in handling the largest ships.

The Commission of Navigation was composed of marine men,

[5] Ammen to Secretary of State, June 21, 1879, *Sen. Doc. 102*, p. 2, 58th Cong., 2d sess. (U.S.).

[6] Isthmian Canal Commission (hereafter designated as I.C.C.), *Report, 1899–1901*, II, 6 (U.S.).

with Dr. O. J. Broch, an ex-minister of Norway, presiding. It studied the questions of winds and currents and the canal's probable effect on shipbuilding, and considered a lock canal acceptable only if a sea-level type were proved impossible. In the event a lock canal were adopted, it reported that expected traffic would require "double locks, side by side, one for vessels going west and the other for vessels going east."

Most fundamental of the committees was the Technical Commission, to which were assigned men who were the most eminent engineers of their time, including Alexandre T. Lavalley and Abel Couvreux, Jr., the dredgers of Suez.

Advocates of the various canal ideas submitted their plans. Francisco de Garay, Mexican delegate, championed Tehuantepec, which was summarily rejected because of its one hundred twenty locks plus twelve days required for transit. United States representatives, Admiral Daniel Ammen, Commander Edward P. Lull, and Civil Engineer A. G. Menocal, proposed a Nicaragua lock canal. The French naval officers, Wyse and Réclus, offered their plan for a sea-level canal at Panamá. Nathan Appleton advocated the thirty-three-mile San Blas route, but it contained a nine-mile tunnel and was rejected. Commander Thomas O. Selfridge suggested a project by way of the Atrato River, and that was rejected. Altogether fourteen plans were submitted. These were sifted down by a subcommittee to two: Nicaragua and Panamá, each with its adherents.

The Technical Commission of the Congress checked upon the distinctive features of these two routes, weighing the merits of the sea-level plan at Panamá and the lock plan at Nicaragua. The inspiration and will of De Lesseps were reported as predominant, and the discussions "long, and sometimes very heated." At its last meeting on May 28 the Technical Commission adopted its findings by vote, recommending a sea-level canal in a route from Colón to Panamá. The vote, however, was not unanimous, and opposition to De Lesseps' sea-level ideas was indicated by abstentions as well as by nays.

With four reports completed, the Ways and Means Commission under the presidency of M. Paul Cérésole, ex-President of the Swiss Confederation, was able to report the "sum of elements of transit" as sufficient to pay the cost of the canal and that it would expand to "an incalculable extent." The transit dues were placed at 15 francs per ton, and an annual net profit of 1,680,000 francs was predicted. This Commission also hoped with the others that, even at a cost of more time and money, the canal could be constructed "without locks or tunnels."

Though all the Commissions reported for a sea-level canal, there were marked differences of opinion, particularly among the engineers. One of them, Adolphe Godin de Lépinay, made a strong plea for a lock-type canal. Of the French members he was the only one who had supervised construction work on the Isthmus. He knew its topography, the nature of the torrential Chagres and the necessity of controlling it. He understood the problem of labor in the tropics and had seen the effects of tropical diseases.

De Lépinay explained that there was a central highland to be crossed by the canal and that excavating a sea-level canal through that mass of land would be too vast a project to undertake in any country, but especially in Panamá where there was yellow fever. He had a simpler and less expensive solution for building the waterway. He knew that the headwaters of the two important Isthmian rivers approached each other near Culebra. The Rio Grande drained southerly into the Pacific; the Obispo drained northerly into the Chagres, which in turn drained into the Atlantic. The valleys of these rivers were bordered by ranges of mountains and hills that provided natural impounding perimeters for the formation of lakes. That was the key to the problem.

It was not strange that, in arriving at his solution for constructing a canal across the mountains, De Lépinay should have utilized the contours of the land and the water supply of the rivers as offering the best means of overcoming the greatest

problems—the control of the Chagres River and the excavating
of a channel across the mountains. He was confident of the
soundness of his plan, which he had first thought of as early as
1859.[7]
De Lépinay's concept of the Panama Canal was of unbeliev-
able simplicity. He proposed the creation of a large lake on
each side of the continental divide by erecting a dam across the
Chagres River and another across the Rio Grande, as close to
the seas as configuration of the land permitted. The water in
each lake would be allowed to rise to the approximate level of
80 feet, the two lakes would be joined by a channel across the
divide, and on each side of the Isthmus locks would be constructed between the lakes and the sea level. His concept is
clear, simple, and definite—a high-level lake on each side of
the Isthmus, joined by an open channel through the mountains,
and each lake connected by locks to the seas.[8] That was the
terminal-lake conception. It was the fundamental plan for
constructing the Panama Canal that has immortalized its origi-
nator.

Unfortunately, the members of that Congress did not understand his prophetic words. In their ignorance of the problem
involved, they could not understand. To them these prophecies
were probably nothing more than engineering abstractions. De
Lépinay's proposal was not even discussed seriously. But failure to understand and approve deprived the French of the only
plan that would have been feasible.

When the voting came, De Lépinay was much perturbed and
rose in protest. He did not want his name linked with what he
called the disastrous measure of the sea-level canal. Defeat could
not shake his confidence in his own concept; for, he said, "If I
have not known how to make my advice triumph, I cannot let it
be believed that I abandon it, all unknown though I am."[9]

[7] L. W. Bates, *Statement*, March 10, 1906 (Hearings No. 18, II, 1666) (U.S.).
[8] Bunau-Varilla, *Panama: the Creation, Destruction, and Resurrection*, p. 26.
[9] De Lépinay; quoted in Bates, *op. cit.*, pp. 1666–67.

He stated the advantages of the lock canal as costing 500,-000,000 francs less than the sea-level, as affording more rapid transit than the sea-level canal, and as avoiding the unnecessary sacrifice of thousands of men. Then he added: "In order not to burden my conscience with these useless deaths and with the loss of a large capital, I abstain from voting, or I vote *No*."[10]

Read today in the light of greater general knowledge, De Lépinay's plan seems so sound and so simple that it is hard to understand how it could have been so completely ignored. Its adoption would have eliminated almost all excavation in the valleys of the Chagres and Rio Grande for the French Canal, except in the sea-level sections. It would have tremendously reduced the quantity of excavation in the Obispo valley and in Culebra Cut. It was, in the main, the canal plan finally adopted in 1906 by the United States.

In a hall crowded with enthusiasts, a vote was taken on the final resolution on May 29 in full session. Summarized, it called for a "one level"[11] canal from Limon Bay to the Bay of Panamá. The vote on this resolution was significant. Of the 135 members, 37 were absent; of the remaining 98, the vote was: ayes 78, nays 8, and 12 not voting. Admiral Ammen refused to vote, on the ground that only engineers should vote. Of the members, 74 were French and 11 were from the United States; 42 were engineers. Of the 78 ayes, 20 were engineers, but only one of them had visited Panamá. Of the 11 United States delegates, 4 were absent, 4 did not vote, and 3 voted for Panamá, Commander Selfridge among the last.

By this vote the Congress had approved a sea-level canal on a location from Limon Bay to Panamá, along a route "traced by Lloyd, Totten, Garella, Wyse and Réclus," at a cost of 1,070,-000,000 francs ($214,000,000), with twelve years' time to complete it. But even so, it appears that a majority of the engineers were skeptical of the sea-level idea. One of them, M.

[10] Congrès International d'Études du Canal Interocéanique, *Compte Rendu des Séances*, pp. 658–59 (tr.).

[11] De Lesseps, *op. cit.*, II, 198–99.

Charles Kleitz, supported his negative vote with the statement that the resolution submitted was "too positive and too absolute." He agreed that the canal should run from Limon Bay to Panamá, but considered the surveys insufficiently thorough to make a choice of type "based upon reasons and proofs."[12] Although he admitted the desirability of a sea-level canal, he considered a lock canal would meet requirements. But of course it would have taken more than the cautious analyses of a few keen engineers to stem the tide in such a well-managed affair.

De Lesseps had lent the full force of his high prestige toward securing a vote for the sea-level canal, deliberately ignoring the technical advice of the well-informed engineer, Godin de Lépinay; but he was supported in his stand for a sea-level canal by the other engineers. Even so, it was at this point that he made a fundamental error in launching the vast program based upon false assumptions.

De Lesseps must have had a sense of high elation as the results were announced. He commended the Congress for its work with highest praise, and yielded the chair to Admiral Baron de la Roncière-le Noury. The Admiral ended an effective closing speech with the hope that "the illustrious gentleman who had been the soul of the deliberations, who was the personification of grand enterprises, and who had charmed all by his courtesy and dignity, might live to witness the completion of the great work to which his name would remain forever attached, and of which he could not refuse to take the direction."

The Great Frenchman could not resist this stirring accolade and replied that "a general who has once gained a battle never refused to engage in another."[13]

ORGANIZING THE PANAMA CANAL COMPANY

In Panamá the people were overjoyed at the news of the approval of the Wyse-Réclus route by the Paris Congress and

[12] I.C.C., op. cit., II, 7 (U.S.).
[13] Panama Star and Herald, June 10, 1879.

that De Lesseps had proclaimed he could raise $100,000,000 in thirty days to commence work.

In the United States, part of the press assumed an ominous tone, threatening to apply the Monroe Doctrine—a tone which was reflected very soon in the Congress of the United States by the introduction on June 25, 1879, of a joint resolution by General Ambrose E. Burnside, "That the people of these States would not view without serious disquietude any attempt by the powers of Europe to establish under their protection and domination a ship-canal across the Isthmus of Darien" and that it would be regarded "as a manifestation of an unfriendly disposition toward the United States."[14]

In France the idea of building another great canal fitted in with the spirit of the time, dimly persistent from the doctrine by Saint-Simon, "social regeneration through work, and universal peace through great public undertakings, and particularly by developing communications between the peoples of the world."[15] There was also the natural desire for a peaceful revenge against the Germans, who had defeated the French so decisively in the Franco-Prussian War.

But how to organize and finance an enterprise so great? Suez had been financed through subscriptions. De Lesseps decided that the same method was best for Panama. This way was independent of capricious government policies, "leaving the enterprise its purely industrial character, and avoiding anything like dabbling in politics."[16] In his efforts to finance Suez he "had walked out on Rothschild," but he had succeeded. Could he repeat it here?

De Lesseps was no longer a young man, having passed his seventy-third birthday. Friends and family tried to dissuade him from heading an undertaking that would require such tremendous efforts and so much time. The difficulties were fore-

[14] Burnside, "Joint Resolution (Sen. Res. No. 43)." *Congressional Record,* IX, Pt. 2, p. 2312 (46th Cong., 1st sess.) (U.S.).

[15] André Siegfried, *Suez and Panama,* p. 239.

[16] De Lesseps, *op. cit.,* II, 178.

seen, and he was warned by the leaders of the risks to be run. For him money was not a motive, as he had sufficient; but it was the glory of a second great victory. His son, Charles de Lesseps, asked ".... for us who have worked at your side, are we to have no repose?"[17] But to all who opposed his assumption of leadership, Ferdinand de Lesseps was deaf. He was confident of success at Panamá, publicly stating that the canal would be completed in eight years at a cost of about $50,000,000 and that the difficulties were "not so formidable as those which had to be overcome in the construction of the Suez Canal, as a railway already exists along the course .... with a large town at each extremity."[18] Some of his statement was true!

To launch such an enormous undertaking the force of a great prestige was needed. In France De Lesseps was regarded as one who had held aloof from the controversies of the canal until he was certain and who would not attempt anything not genuine or feasible beyond a doubt. He would expect to make money, but being rich already he needed no more; besides, at seventy-four a man with his record could not be moved by a financial consideration. The motive was "fame rather than greed for gold."

The Universal Interoceanic Panama Canal Company (Compagnie Universelle du Canal Interocéanique de Panama), now known as the Old Panama Canal Company, was started with a capital stock of 400,000,000 francs ($80,000,000)—800,000 shares at 500 francs each; and it was speedily announced that De Lesseps would dig the first spade of earth on January 1, 1880. De Lesseps at first proposed General Grant as the first honorary president, while he himself would serve as general manager; but opposition in the United States did not permit, and De Lesseps was made president.

It was necessary to obtain money for organizing the new company. This was done by selling 400 founders' shares of 5,000 francs each to persons "interested in the creation of great enterprises,"[19] to each of whom were given free 100 additional shares. Thus was obtained 2,000,000 francs ($400,000). De Lesseps then acquired the Wyse Concession from the society headed by General Türr, for the high price of 10,000,000 francs ($2,000,-000). A public subscription was arranged for August 6 and 7, and circulars were sent out to Europe and America announcing the formation of the company, with an expected annual income of 90,000,000 francs and dividends at the rate of 11.5 per cent.

Strong political attacks on the effort marked the opening of the campaign. The cost estimates were considered too small and estimated receipts too great. Both the press and the high financial circles in France were hostile. The subscription tended to arouse fears in the United States, which were increased by the campaign for Nicaragua by Admiral Ammen and Civil Engineer Menocal. De Lesseps was represented as a Bonapartist seeking power.

Why all this opposition arose was not clear at the time; but many years later, after the collapse of the company and when Charles de Lesseps was being prosecuted, he claimed that his father succeeded in stopping the clamor of the opposition by placing the financial management of the company in charge of a small group associated with "journalism and finance, who undertook to render public opinion favorable to the enterprise."[20] That was the price De Lesseps had to pay for the privilege of being left alone.

The result of the first campaign was almost a complete failure, with only 30,000,000 francs ($6,000,000) subscribed; but it did not deter De Lesseps. In August, although admitting the failure, he called for new surveys and the sending to Panamá of an International Technical Commission of celebrated engineers, which he would accompany, to check the Panamá location as the most practicable route. Then by visiting the United States in person he would "silence the clamor of opposition raised by hostile America." It should be remembered that the press in the United

---

[19] Siegfried, *op. cit.*, p. 244. [20] I.C.C., *op. cit.*, II, 8 (U.S.).

States had become so active as to surprise and startle not only
France but also Panamá, where the people thought the United
States was playing at Panamá the part played by England at
Suez when De Lesseps was so bitterly opposed. But they hoped
he would be equally successful in his second battle. They believed the "reckless adventurer condemned by the English Press
is today the great genius whose energy and foresight have carried out the greatest work of our country, in spite of a seemingly
insurmountable opposition."[21]

To assist in overcoming opposition to the Panama Canal idea,
De Lesseps started a fortnightly bulletin on September 1, 1879,
entitled *Bulletin du Canal Interocéanique,* which was published
until February 1889. It issued promotional propaganda and
reports on construction during the French effort and probably
inspired later the starting of the *Canal Record* by the Isthmian
Canal Commission in 1907. The result of the opposition was to
delay, but not to defeat, the French efforts.

ECHOES IN THE UNITED STATES AND PANAMA

At regular intervals during these early promotional periods
there appeared some strongly realistic persons. They had spoken
during the Paris Congress in May. From New York came ideas
from Colonel Totten, then an old man. After completing the
Panama Railroad, he had studied the canal problem and submitted a plan in 1857 for a lock canal from Limon Bay to Panamá Bay. Its main features called for a bottom width of 150
feet, a depth of 31 feet, locks 400 by 30 feet, and a summit level
of 150 feet supplied by a 24-mile feeder from the upper Chagres.
The estimated cost was $80,000,000.[22]

Naturally he watched the Paris proceedings intently and published his views. Writing in October 1879, he pointed out that
up to the end of the Congress the type of the canal considered
necessary was doubtful, that is, whether it should be sea-level,

21 *Panama Star and Herald,* Sept. 7, 1879.
22 J. E. Nourse, *The Maritime Canal of Suez,* p. 142 (U.S.).

lock, or tunnel, but it had been decided that Panamá was the most advantageous route. At this time Colonel Totten considered a sea-level canal impracticable from the business standpoint. He did not mean, however, that with enough "money, science and perseverance" it could not have been accomplished.

The sea-level plan of Wyse and Réclus provided a dam for the Chagres—the river whose sudden floods created the greatest of problems for the sea-level plan. This problem, he thought, could be handled only by diverting the Chagres in a "radical removal," for damming the river was considered too dangerous. Totten was familiar with the features of the country and had no illusions. Based upon a bottom width of 105 feet in earth and 120 feet in rock, he estimated a cost for a sea-level type at $344,000,000 without a tunnel. To this he added $85,000,000 for diverting the Chagres to Las Minas Bay, bringing the total to $429,000,000—a cost so great as to cause him to consider a sea-level canal impracticable.[23]

In the meantime plans went forward for the approaching visit to Panamá of the International Technical Commission. De Lesseps conducted a lecture tour of France, and every mail to the Isthmus brought news from France of new indications of the "earnestness and sincerity" of De Lesseps in his great work of uniting the oceans. In November word came that he expected to arrive late the following month.

The program of opposition in the United States continued undiminished, but United States citizens in Panamá remained sympathetic to the French. All looked forward to the coming visit of De Lesseps, predicting that the "intelligence, energy and good faith" which he had used in "making.the Panamá route known to the world, and of inaugurating actual work in the enterprise" would prove of "more value than the lucubrations of a dozen politicians, presidents though they be."[24]

During the fall of 1879 a party of engineers from France ar-

23 *Panama Star and Herald*, Dec. 9, 1879.
24 *Ibid.*, Dec. 4, 1879.

rived at Panamá with drilling machines. They began a series of borings and surveys in preparation for the consulting engineers. A special reception committee arranged a schedule of entertainment for the distinguished guests, among whom were expected Wyse and Réclus, and Colonel Totten, the builder of the Panama Railroad.

As the time for De Lesseps' arrival approached, the Isthmians increased their confidence in the future as well as their disdain for North Americans. The latter had been "maundering and drivelling over their Monroe Doctrine, and the necessity of American supremacy in a part of the world where their interests are fifth rate," while De Lesseps was "working quietly and practically, demonstrating the first part of the great problem,"[25] that is, the practicability of the route from Limon Bay to Panamá and the cost of construction. That was the spirit at Panamá almost on the eve of the arrival of the Great Frenchman.

DE LESSEPS ARRIVES AT PANAMA

On the afternoon of December 30, 1879, an excited crowd was waiting on a wharf in Colón. The city was decorated with flags of all nations except the United States. A band was playing "soul-stirring airs," and the reception committee gathered as the "Lafayette," flagship of the French West Indies Squadron, approached her berth. As soon as the gangway was rigged the reception committee went to the saloon and greeted Ferdinand de Lesseps. With him were his young wife and three young children, whom he had brought as the best way to discredit the accepted rumors about the dangers of the Panamá climate. Also there were eminent engineers of the International Technical Commission, who had come with him from France, and a group from the United States, which included Nathan Appleton, of Boston; Trenor W. Park, President of the Panama Railroad; and Colonel Totten, who served as the important connecting link between the building of the railroad and the French canal effort.

[25] *Ibid.*, Dec. 25, 1879.

An address of welcome was made by J. A. Céspedes, with a gracious response by De Lesseps, and afterward came the usual cordialities and convivialities. Tracy Robinson, a member of the committee and long a resident of Colón, has left his impressions of the seventy-four-year-old canal builder. He was "still active and vigorous; a small man, French in detail, with winning manners, and what is called a magnetic presence." He was confident and convincing, answering all questions about the canal with facility and amiability. Robinson asked him, "What will be done with the Chagres River?" Without hestitating he replied, "It is the intention to turn the upper river into the Pacific Ocean, thereby relieving the lower valley of all danger of floods."[26] This conversation made a great impression at the time. It was a new idea.

In the evening there was a display of fireworks from the icehouse, the most popular institution of those days. Later in the evening De Lesseps, with a few friends, went ashore for a stroll around the streets of Colón, among throngs of enthusiastic Isthmians.

The next day was one for work. De Lesseps and the engineers inspected the Pacific Mail wharf. He asked about the force and nature of northers which, because of the northern exposure of Limon Bay, so often had made that anchorage unsafe. He indicated the location of a breakwater and the probable canal entrance on a chart and evidenced complete satisfaction in the prospects for the successful completion of the canal. He recognized only two great difficulties: the Chagres River and the cutting of the canal through the summit at Culebra. The first problem would be overcome by diverting its headwaters "into another channel, and the second will disappear before the wells which will be sunk and charged with explosives of sufficient force to remove vast quantities at each discharge."[27] Landing for the first

[26] Robinson, *Panama: A Personal Record of Forty-six Years, 1861–1907,* pp. 139–40.

[27] *Panama Star and Herald,* Jan. 1, 1880.

time in that region of luxuriant vegetation, just at the beginning of the dry season, before plants had begun to fade, he must have compared the scene with the desert of his former endeavor at uninhabited Suez. It is no wonder that the very existence of the railroad impressed him and that he expected work to start without much delay.

With the visit at Colón completed, he left for Panamá City on the 11:30 A.M. train, and all along the line met scenes which he called "indescribable ovations." When halfway to Panamá, at Barbacoas bridge, the President of the State of Panamá boarded the train and entertained at dinner on the way to Panamá City, where elaborate preparations had been made to honor their illustrious guest.

When the train stopped, the party stepped off into an open tent where the "great impresario" was introduced to all the local dignitaries; from there they were taken in carriages to the Grand Hotel, along the Avenida Central, between lines of Colombian troops. The Avenida Central and connecting streets were profusely decorated, with the flags of France and Colombia prevailing. At intervals were mounted shields, each bearing the name of earlier Isthmian explorers—from Balboa in 1513 to Wyse, Réclus, and Pedro J. Sosa in 1877 and 1878. On arches were salutations—at Santa Ana Plaza one which read "Colombia salutes Ferdinand de Lesseps"; at the Grand Hotel another reading "Panama salutes her illustrious guest, Ferdinand de Lesseps."[28]

His work for the next decade was to be the dominating subject of conversation and thought on the Isthmus and the cause of endless discussion in the United States.

[28] *Ibid.*, Jan. 1, 1880.

Chapter III

PROMOTING THE PANAMA CANAL COMPANY

The United States have, by right, the pre-eminence in this enterprise and it is my conviction they will secure it. Science has declared that the canal is possible, and I am the servant of science. I will carry this work to a successful result, and it will make America queen of the seas.—Ferdinand de Lesseps, builder of the Suez Canal.[1]

DE LESSEPS INAUGURATES THE PANAMA CANAL

During the preceding June, De Lesseps had promised to dig the first spade of earth for the Panama Canal on January 1, 1880. When that day arrived he was at Panamá, ready to carry out his promise in the manner that only a distinguished graduate of the Suez undertaking could have managed. He planned to move the first ground at the mouth of the Rio Grande, the future canal entrance, with his young daughter Ferdinande de Lesseps turning the "first sod."[2]

De Lesseps and his party of distinguished guests boarded the steam tender "Taboguilla" to make the three-mile trip to the Rio Grande, with the intention of landing for a ceremony after a reception and feast on board. The departure was delayed by late guests, and by the time the "Taboguilla" arrived near her destination the waters of the Pacific had receded so far as to prevent the vessel from approaching the desired spot. De Lesseps rose to the occasion and broke out his ceremonial shovel and pickaxe, which he had brought from France especially for the inauguration of the Canal. Announcing that the ceremony was only symbolic, he proceeded to conduct it on board with a champagne box filled with earth. Amid much applause, young Ferdinande struck the first blow with the pickaxe. Then followed

[1] *Addresses at the De Lesseps Banquet, March 1, 1880*, p. 24.
[2] W. C. Haskins, *Canal Zone Pilot*, p. 180.

other symbolic blows by the guests to show, as De Lesseps explained it, the "alliance of all peoples in the work of uniting
the two oceans for the good of mankind."[3]

De Lesseps then proclaimed the fulfillment of his promise
to begin practical work on January 1, 1880, expressed confidence of success in the task to which he had dedicated the closing years of his life, and said he had no fear of lack in financial
assistance for the opening of another great highway of world
trade. There were more speeches, and the exercises were concluded with a benediction by Bishop José T. Paúl of Panamá,
who extended the blessings of the Universal Church. And the
party returned to Panamá.

The third day of the De Lesseps reception was relatively
quiet. There was only an exhibition drill by a battalion of the
Colombian Army. Behind the scenes of gaiety, however, the
International Technical Commission began its laborious work
of exploring and examining the canal route.

The last celebrations for De Lesseps were held on Sunday,
January 4, 1880. There were a military display, some bullfights
in the Plaza Santa Ana, and finally an elaborate banquet for
one hundred forty at the Grand Hotel (now the Panamá Post
Office). There Dr. Antonio Ferro presided, with Madame De
Lesseps sitting on his right and Ferdinand de Lesseps to the
left. Among the guests were the illustrious Bishop Paúl of Panamá, Lucien Wyse, and Colonel Totten. After replying to the
toasts made to him, De Lesseps observed the presence of news-
paper men. Knowing how closely the United States was watching and how much public opinion there was created by the news-
papers, he proposed a toast to the press—"The representatives
of public opinion, the greatest force of our epoch, with the assistance of which the great commercial and interoceanic highway for the benefit of the world would be made in Colombian
territory, under the protection of the Colombian Government,
and of the great powers of the world."

[3] *Canal Record*, July 29, 1908, I, 383 (U.S.).

Later, De Lesseps announced that the International Technical Commission had completed its organization, under the presidency of Colonel Totten and the distinguished canal engineer,
Jacob Dirks of Holland. The canal line from Colón to Panamá
had been divided into five sections, each with a brigade of engineers to conduct surveys. De Lesseps ended by referring to the
important work done for the canal by Wyse, who had negotiated
its concession and explored the route.

Wyse did have firsthand knowledge. He knew how the work
would have to be done in the Panamá climate and, after acknowl-
edging the unusual recognition by his chief, he proposed the
health of "the humble laborers, without distinction of race or
nationality, who in the future may be the useful but modest instruments"[4] to bring the great work to completion. It was evident to him then that the black man would perform the hard labor
in that climate.

All of this prelude appears characterized by a lamentable
artificiality and lack of reality. Some of it was induced by ignorance of the country—its geography, its geology, its climate
and health conditions and resources. Part was due to incorrect
conclusions drawn from the experience of Suez, which unfortunately did not apply at all to the Isthmus of Panamá—a land
which John F. Stevens, as chief engineer of the Panama Canal
for the United States, described about twenty-five years later as
"one of the most forbidding spots on earth"[5] from a construction
viewpoint. Above all, it should be remembered that De Lesseps
was not an engineer but a trained diplomat, that he was the promoter of the most gigantic commercial enterprise in the history
of the world and had taken on himself the task of financing it by
private subscription. Notwithstanding his advanced age, he had
proved himself a gifted propagandist and promoter. By his selection of the Panama route he had determined the location of
the trans-Isthmian waterway and had started one of the greatest
works of man.

[4] *Panama Star and Herald*, Jan. 6, 1880, p. 2.
[5] J. F. Stevens, *An Engineer's Recollections*, p. 40.

SURVEY BY DE LESSEPS AND
INTERNATIONAL TECHNICAL COMMISSION

January is a pleasant month in Panamá, with refreshing trade winds during the day and little or no rain. The rainy season ends in December, and in January the dry season is not advanced enough to present the parched appearance of April; instead, the landscape retains much of the luxuriant green of the rainy days. It was an ideal month for the Technical Commission to start its labors.

This exploring effort was considered in Panamá as the "largest, the most efficient" with respect to experience and practical knowledge of members, "the most completely equipped, and perfectly organized." Besides, it had the "advantage of being under the leadership of a veteran campaigner, whose name is a guarantee of success."[6]

The exploring parties, at first organized into five groups, were changed later to eight, each under a competent engineer. Reports of observations made in the field were forwarded to the commission headquarters in Panamá, where they were classified by a committee consisting of Colonel Totten, Mr. Dirks, and General W. W. Wright, for use in the final report. De Lesseps remained conveniently near in Panamá with Wyse and kept in close touch with the progress of the survey.

De Lesseps had already inaugurated the canal at the mouth of the Rio Grande. He next decided to inaugurate the excavation of Culebra Cut on January 10, 1880, and went to Cerro Culebra (afterward known as Gold Hill) for the ceremony. A mine, fitted with an electric firing device, had been laid in the hard basalt formation a few feet below the summit and was ready. Proceeding with some celebrities, including Bishop Paúl and little Ferdinande, he again selected the daughter to render the honors. The Bishop extended his blessing, and Ferdinande pressed the button. Large masses of rock were hurled into the

---

[6] *Panama Star and Herald*, Jan. 7, 1880. Jan. 29, 1880.

air, and the party returned to Panama enthusiastic for the
"perfect success."[7]

The work outlined for the International Technical Commission was large. It comprised a verification of all previous surveys, including those of Lull and Menocal and also of Wyse and
Réclus, the making of necessary additional surveys, and the
final determination of the line of the canal. Borings had to be
made to determine the nature of the earth along the canal line
and at terminal ports. Calculations of quantities to be excavated and classification of materials were required, along with
cost estimates. All of this was necessary to enable preparation
of working plans for the Wyse-Réclus sea-level canal, which De
Lesseps unfortunately thought feasible at a much smaller cost
than was estimated originally. Special attention was paid to
the Chagres and to the geology of the Isthmus. The earth depth
was found to be greater and the rock softer than at first supposed.
The Technical Commission also re-examined the project of
erecting a dam at Gamboa and the diversion of the Chagres. It
hoped by investigating and reporting on these matters that De
Lesseps, when he arrived in New York, would be supplied with
information to refute charges that he was simply a "promoter
of a work hastily conceived, whose difficulties are but half understood, whose plans are imperfect, and its estimates of cost
unreliable."[8] All this was necessary to combat the propaganda
for Nicaragua, headed by Ammen and Menocal in the United
States, and also for use in later financial campaigns. Even so,
the few weeks' time allowed for the survey was too short for an
investigation of such vast importance.

Like the sudden influx of canal workers in later years, the
arrival of the French engineers in the small community of the
Isthmus had its effects. Prices advanced suddenly. Merchants
were seized with a "mania of sudden riches." Rent soared from
$40 per month to $80. Vacant lots formerly priced at $1,000

[7] *Panama Star and Herald*, Jan. 12, 1880.
[8] *Ibid.*, Jan. 29, 1880.

sold at $4,000. People thought that the French had come with pockets bulging with gold and willing to give without receiving any value.

The rise in prices was reported to the home office of the company. As a result, ready-made houses were ordered from Chicago, and the Canal Company embarked on a policy of establishing its own towns. The dangers to the business interests of Panamá then were recognized by the press, which previously had accepted the canal work as an assured fact with a great expenditure of money certain. It warned, however, against expecting a "reckless expenditure," frankly stating that if the Panamanians would give real value then "well and good, if they will not, then this immense company can easily and will readily provide for themselves."

The report of the International Commission was ready on February 14, with replies to the questions which De Lesseps had asked of them. The line of the canal recommended by the Paris Congress was verified, and slight changes were made to reduce curvature. Borings to depths of 12 to 21 meters had been taken along the line of the canal and at the Gamboa Dam site. To produce stable banks on the sides of the canal the Commission adopted a slope of 1 to 1 for all excavations, except the summit division, where a slope of ¼ to 1 was recommended.

In general the canal was to be a trench 72 feet wide at the bottom and 27½ feet deep, on a route following the Panama Railroad. Starting at Colón, the canal would pass through six miles of lowlands to the Chagres valley at Gatun. It would then follow the valley for about 21 miles to Gamboa, where it would curve right and follow the valley of the Obispo, cross the continental divide at Culebra, and join the Pacific by following the valley of the Rio Grande.

Unless something was done to control the Chagres, a sea-level canal would have caused a huge waterfall from the higher bed of the Chagres into the canal at Gamboa. Accordingly there were planned a giant dam 40 meters high to retain its waters in a large lake, and a new channel, the east diversion, to carry its waters to the Atlantic. For drainage on the opposite side there would have to be a west diversion. South of the cordillera an east and a west diversion would have to be constructed, thus making a total of five canals—one main canal and four diversion channels. For terminal facilities no work was considered necessary, except a tidal lock at the Pacific where the tidal range was great, and a breakwater at Colón where the anchorage was subject to heavy northers. The grand total excavation was estimated at 75,000,000 cubic meters, and the estimate of total cost was 843,000,000 francs ($168,600,000), a much higher figure than that of the Paris Congress, which did not cover items for interest and miscellaneous expenses totaling 409,000,000 francs. The report, signed by all members with Colonel Totten's name at the head of the list, was later described by J. B. Bishop as thorough and scientific. It declared that with "good and judicious management"[9] the canal could be completed within eight years.

With completion of the survey, the time for De Lesseps' departure had arrived. During his visit he had endeared himself to the people of the Isthmus. Gracious, affable, and courtly, he was well liked and he liked people. A splendid horseman, he was admired as he rode over the trails on his inspections. At no time did the volume or importance of his work prevent him and his wife from infusing "new vigor and animation" into the dull life of the Isthmus. He cultivated his Panamá friends. He attended their churches and social affairs. He sympathized with them in sorrow and became the godfather of their children. He worked all day and danced all night with the energy of a youth, one time even crossing the Isthmus with Colonel Totten to attend a ball given in their honor.

It was only natural, when the time came for De Lesseps to leave Panamá, that the departure of this extraordinary man was as spectacular as his arrival, the same state committee accom-

[9] *Panama Star and Herald*, Feb. 16, 1880.

panying him across the Isthmus. While at Colón he selected the
permanent site for the statue of Columbus, presented to Colombia by Empress Eugénie of France, and received new ovations
and honors.

When mentioning the work of his International Technical
Commission, he declared that with its report in his hands the
raising of the necessary funds in France would be "less onerous
than the labor of gathering together the millions which gave the
Suez Canal to the commerce of the world."[10]

On Sunday, February 15, 1880, shortly after the ceremonies
for the Columbus statue, he boarded the "S.S. Colon" and left
for New York, having been on the Isthmus one month and seven-
teen days.

DE LESSEPS VISITS THE UNITED STATES

On the voyage to New York De Lesseps studied the report of
the engineers and revised the estimates of construction costs
downward from their 843,000,000 francs ($168,600,000) to
656,000,000 francs ($131,200,000).[11] Having just seen the
problems of the Isthmus by personal observation and received
the technical report of the survey by his Commission, he must
have known that great difficulties were ahead. His action in reducing the estimates is hard to understand except on the basis
that he was preparing a promotional campaign which he wanted
to wage in the United States. The object was success, not ac-
curacy.

His arrival in the United States was anticipated with a tremendous, but somewhat hostile, public interest. A committee
met his steamer and escorted him to his hotel for too brief a
rest; and he was again on his campaign, opened by an address
on March 1, 1880, before the American Society of Civil Engineers.

As he started to explain the canal, his map fell suddenly to

10 *Ibid.*
11 J. B. Bishop, *The Panama Gateway*, p. 75.

the floor. Quickly he exclaimed: "Oh, there's my canal gone to the ground!" It was picked up immediately and replaced. De Lesseps, gracious and quick, remarked: "But America has restored it to me," and continued unperturbed. Though pleased to be received and acclaimed as an engineer, he did not want any misunderstanding about himself or his background and explained that his training had been as a diplomat and not as an engineer.

As to the original capital of the company, he wanted it understood that one-half could be subscribed in the United States, as he knew that the interests of the United States in the canal were vital, equaling "all the rest of the world put together."

De Lesseps' determination for a sea-level canal came out strongly on this occasion. Someone in the audience asked why a lock canal should not be constructed instead of a sea-level canal as recommended by the Commission. The response was instant: "If the committee had decided to build a lock canal I would have put on my hat and gone home."[12] This won the audience, and he ended the meeting with new friends created for Panama.

The same evening he was lionized in the typical North American way at a banquet at Delmonico's, the most famous New York restaurant of the time. Adorned with flowers and flags, the dining room made an effective setting for the coats of arms of the United States and France as well as the models of Suez and Panama. The guests numbered 253 carefully selected leaders and their ladies, from the financial, religious, diplomatic, and political fields in the United States.

In an eloquent and interesting speech of welcome, the distinguished clergyman, Richard S. Storrs, presented a word picture of the importance of communications in the cause of peace, telling how De Lesseps had planned not only the Suez Canal but the Corinth Canal and the railroad from Europe to India. He mentioned the German geographer, Johannes Schoener, the namer of America, who constructed a globe in 1520 clearly

[12] *Panama Star and Herald,* March 12, 1880.

showing the Isthmus of Panamá with a line drawn across it as if to represent a future Strait of Panama[13]—probably the first map of its kind. He was impressed at the sight of that man of seventy-four setting forth to realize the dream of three and one-half centuries as the crowning achievement of his long life. The distinguished diplomat, John Bigelow, likewise supported De Lesseps as the natural leader and ridiculed the idea of the French effort being a violation of the Monroe Doctrine. If aiding commerce by digging a canal were a violation, he said, "we are violating it every day in permitting our railway bonds to be sold abroad and foreign steamers to land and unload at our wharves."[14]

De Lesseps replied in French. Realizing the nature of opposition which had been rising in the United States, he endeavored to remove its cause. He explained that in negotiating with Colombia he had announced that he had no political interest, nor did he seek to advance the interests of France. If the canal should become a political issue he declared he would be "very happy to have recourse to the protection of the United States."[15] This same declaration, he said, would be made also to the President of the United States when he visited Washington.

There were many other speeches before the close of that long evening. The guests were interested in Panama, but more interested in De Lesseps. They were struck with the "magnificent freshness, enterprise, and youth" of the man who sat there "crowned with the triumph of a desperate but successful victory,"[16] in overcoming deserts of Africa and joining the waters of the Mediterranean with those of the Red Sea. They wanted to see that ability and experience applied to Panama.

In Washington, De Lesseps called on President Hayes. In an interview afterward he reported the meeting as having been highly satisfactory; but soon afterward President Hayes, not in-

[13] *Addresses at the De Lesseps Banquet, March 1, 1880,* p. 15.
[14] *Ibid.,* p. 20.   [15] *Ibid.,* p. 24.
[16] Address by H. W. Bellows, *ibid.,* p. 46.

fluenced by De Lesseps' call nor by the speeches at Delmonico's, sent a strong message to the Senate on March 8, 1880, calling for a "canal under American control," and declaring that the United States could not consent to "the surrender of this control to any European power or to any combination of European powers."[17] The Government of the United States had not forgotten the ill-fated dream of an empire in Mexico which France had attempted to realize only twenty years before in the tragic episode of Maximilian. But, as John Bigelow pointed out in his speech at Delmonico's, if there were any fears of violation of the Monroe Doctrine, the fate of Maximilian in Mexico should have ended them.

While in Washington De Lesseps also appeared before a congressional committee, dealing with the canals. He expressed his delight with the presidential message, saying it certainly would be "advantageous to have the protection of the United States during the work and after the opening of the canal."[18] To his *Bulletin* in Paris he telegraphed that the President's message "assured the safety of the canal."

Indications of a favorable public reaction were almost immediate. De Lesseps' visit was hailed as the most publicly appreciated visit of a foreigner in over twenty years. He was acclaimed as a prophet of the incoming era of world-wide commerce and national intercourse. "With the eagle glance of genius he stands upon the summit where the rising dawn casts its earliest light, and sees, in advance of the sleepers in the shadowed valleys below, the illumination which the climbing sun will shed upon them also."[19] The favorable reactions in the United States were most gratifying to those left behind in Panamá and to those who were watching from Paris.

Like so many less disinterested propagandists since that time, De Lesseps toured the United States. He visited San Francisco,

---

[17] *Messages and Papers of the Presidents,* X, 4537–38 (U.S.).

[18] *Panama Star and Herald,* March 23, 1880.

[19] *New York Herald,* March 3, 1880.

Boston, Chicago, and other cities. In some his receptions were not so favorable as in New York. In Chicago he met some opposition, which exasperated him. He was addressing a large crowd at the Exchange when someone confronted him with that ubiquitous question—the Monroe Doctrine. Boldly he answered the challenging heckler: "Here are 20,000 of you Americans. Now explain to me how the Monroe Doctrine prevents my making the canal." There was silence. He must have known that they did not have an accurate understanding of that famed doctrine. He then explained the meaning of the Monroe Doctrine and that it did not operate against building the canal. He added: "I cannot agree with a town only one-third my own age, though with 400,000 inhabitants, which says that the thing is impossible."[20]

"Hurrah! That's the boy we want!" was the instinctive response of the audience. He had won another victory.

Returning to New York after his wearing trip, he did not take long for rest. The following morning there was a reception and luncheon at the home of Cyrus W. Field, of trans-Atlantic cable fame. In the afternoon he was again interviewed by the press. He announced that shares to the value of 300,000,-000 francs (600,000 shares at 500 francs) would be offered in the United States as soon as arrangements could be made in Paris for the formation of a banking syndicate in the United States. Should the United States take that amount, De Lesseps said, she would have a "controlling voice in the enterprise." But in event no shares at all were sold, he said, he would still build his canal, for he was confident of his success because he had a market for his securities in Europe. He declared: "In France and England I am confident I can place all the shares if America does not wish to take any; but from my reception here I am of the opinion that the United States will be inclined to take a large proportion of them. At any rate I shall proceed with my canal."[21]

20 *Panama Star and Herald*, Dec. 28, 1880.
21 *Ibid.*, April 21, 1880.

The next day, April 2, 1880, the De Lesseps family was taken to the White Star liner "Adriatic" by Cyrus Field. They sailed for France via England, Belgium, and Holland with a send-off that equaled their arrival in enthusiasm. However, De Lesseps had not been able to sell his securities in the country he had just toured and from which he had received such extensive honors and universal genuine admiration. But he had made friends.

THE CAMPAIGN FOR PANAMA IN EUROPE

Upon arrival at Liverpool he reopened the promotion campaign. He proposed the offer of £166,000 worth of shares to the British public and publicly estimated that 8,000 men could complete the work in six years—a rash statement for a promoter of a project of the enormous magnitude of the Panama Canal.

De Lesseps was a captivating speaker. People instinctively believed what he said. While at Brussels he announced that the work of digging the canal would be undertaken by Messrs. Couvreux and Hersent, the contractors who had helped him so much at Suez. Bunau-Varilla suggests that this talk, notable for its large number of errors, gives an interesting insight into the views of De Lesseps, who did not like engineers. He had had to arbitrate their disputes too often at Suez. He did like practical men, and Couvreux was a "practical man." The result was that De Lesseps, overconfident already because of his earlier successes and prestige, was convinced that the building of the Panama Canal was an easy task. Convincing De Lesseps was the same as convincing France. He did not realize that, with "new elements of labour, new sanitary conditions, excess of rainfall, and ground to excavate the nature of which was unknown," serious error could result from the advice of men whose "limited education deprives them of that suppleness of mind needed to foresee and to measure the unknown quantities in a new problem."[22]

De Lesseps was followed by Abel Couvreux, Jr., who said

[22] Bunau-Varilla, *Panama: The Creation, Destruction, and Resurrection,* pp. 28–32.

his firm would undertake the construction at an estimate of 512,000,000 francs ($102,400,000). This was a figure still further reducing the inadequate estimates, which he explained was possible because of improvements made in excavating and boring machinery. Couvreux and Hersent wanted eight years to complete the work—two for organization, surveys, and assembly of material and six for the main work on the line of the canal. More than twenty years later it required about three years' preparatory work and seven years' construction for the United States to complete the canal with machinery vastly superior to that of 1880.

In that summer De Lesseps toured the cities of France. Speaking in the interest of the approaching subscription, he informed the public that the International Technical Commission had investigated the canal line on the Isthmus and declared it practicable; also that the work would be undertaken by Couvreux and Hersent, the contractors who had proved their ability at Suez, who estimated that eight years were required for completion.[23] The annual traffic, he prophesied, would be 6,000,-000 tons and produce a revenue of 90,000,000 francs. His prophecy of tonnage was justified.

Late in the summer of 1880 came reports from the United States that financial obstacles were being resolved. The difficulties of winning American capitalists and public confidence were overcome by securing three bankers to form a committee in New York: J. and W. Seligman & Co.; Drexel, Morgan & Company; and Winslow, Lanier & Company. Secretary of the Navy Richard W. Thompson resigned his Cabinet post to accept a position at the head of this committee at the attractive salary of $25,000 and to become a promoter for the Panama Canal Company.

However, in the United States it still looked as if the subscription were being unduly delayed, but this delay was explained as a desire of the Panama Canal Company to await the

[23] I.C.C., *Report, 1899–1901*, II, 12 (U.S.).

opening of the United States Congress. It was reported that De Lesseps expected no opposition from the United States Government and was not apprehensive of any interference with his plans.

At last came the announcement. The Panama stock would be offered in December. The promotion was undertaken vigorously. The movement became so universal as to insure success. All countries in Europe were reported as taking part. Offices were opened in Germany, Austria, Italy, and England. In the *Bulletin du Canal* of November 15 the definite announcement was made that the subscription would take place on December 6, 7, and 8, 1880.

The capital structure was described as 600,000 shares at 500 francs each, totaling 300,000,000 francs, with 590,000 shares available for the public and only 10,000 shares reserved for founders—the result of De Lesseps' desire to encourage the small investors. Suez shareholders were to have a preference, with one share of Panama stock allowed for each share of Suez held. The subscription was announced as covering only half the cost of the canal, of which the total cost was estimated to be 600,000,000 francs.

The *Bulletin* of November 15, 1880, quoted a letter from De Lesseps answering the arguments of his critics, which he placed in two classes. To those who presented false estimates to prove the enterprise could not pay, he stated that Couvreux and Hersent, the contractors of Suez, were going at the moment to Panamá to make new studies for undertaking the work. As for those who wished to inspire fear of the United States, he simply referred them to the successful trip from which he had just returned.[24]

In one of his many press conferences held a few days before the subscription, De Lesseps was highly elated at the favorable news coming in from all directions and at the subscriptions "flowing in" from the United States. He had a greater confi-

[24] *Panama Star and Herald*, Dec. 14, 1880.

dence in Panamá than he had had in Suez and enthusiastically classed the Isthmus as a "wonderful country," where "the Atlantic and Pacific breezes blowing over it will make it the healthiest region in the world. We were there for months—my wife, children, friends, and laborers—and we had not a single death."[25] Then, with a rare sense of unreality, he referred to the reservoir which he planned to receive the waters of the Chagres, thus providing water "to irrigate 500,000 hectares of waste land"—this in a land which has one of the greatest annual rainfalls in the world. Thereupon he invited his interviewer to attend the opening with him in 1887—words that were echoed over the world!

THE RESPONSE IN FRANCE

The lack of financial interest shown in the United States was more than compensated by the exceptional enthusiasm and support in France. When the subscriptions were closed on the ninth of December, the public had subscribed 600,000,000 francs— more than twice the offering. He had succeeded in interesting the small investors—the shopkeepers and peasants of France. De Lesseps was the idol of Suez. He had kept Suez in the hands of many stockholders instead of the financial hierarchy. Panamá would be another Suez.

Plans for organizing the company quickly evolved. To provide financial services a Panama Bank was founded in Paris; to supply food a Commercial Panama Company was organized; and a general meeting of the stockholders of the Canal Company was called for January 31.

This was followed by a second constitutive meeting on March 3, when De Lesseps read his report. It was definite. There were 102,230 shareholders, and the canal was to be completed in 1888. The total excavation was estimated to be between 73,000,-000 and 75,000,000 cubic meters. The total cost of construction was estimated at 512,000,000 francs.

Marine dredges would work at Colón on the Atlantic sea-level

[25] *Ibid.*, Dec. 28, 1880.

section and at La Boca on the Pacific. In the difficult Culebra Cut, work would start in October 1881. Between 8,000 and 10,000 men would be recruited quickly from Colombia and the West Indies to work on the canal, and the canal would be completed.

The picture presented was too simple. It was admitted that De Lesseps was an experienced man, that the railroad along the line of the canal was a tremendous advantage, and that De Lesseps and his project had the good will of the world. But there were some who had misgivings.

The tragic fact remained that De Lesseps was not fundamentally familiar with Panamá. He had not lived there long enough, not even through the cycle of one year. He did not realize that he could not apply all the lessons of Suez to the American Isthmus. Circumstances forced him to stay at home to raise money for the enterprise, while the work was to be carried on so far away that he could not observe closely enough to avoid or correct mistakes. He had underestimated the cost, and right from the first the company was destined to be hard pressed for funds. He would be victimized. Also, he was aging.

The climate which De Lesseps had tried so hard to prove salubrious was in a land endemic with tropical diseases and "notoriously more pestilential than any part of the Desert of Suez." The Government of Colombia, on the surface friendly, was not strong enough to be of any support. On the contrary, it was the cause of much delay and confusion, for the Bogotá politicians looked upon Panamá as the "milch-cow of Colombia."[26] The resources of the region were such that practically all materials and food would have to be imported. But of more importance, all labor would have to be imported, for "In Panama [De Lesseps] has no gangs of Fellaheen forced to work for scant wages, no enthusiastic Khedive willing to command the resources of the State for the benefit of the undertaking."[27]

[26] J. B. and F. Bishop, *Goethals, Genius of the Panama Canal: a Biography,* p. 113.　　　　　　　　　　[27] *London Standard,* Dec. 8, 1880, p. 5.

CHAPTER IV

DE LESSEPS STARTS A SEA-LEVEL CANAL

For [De Lesseps] the sea level canal he had proposed at the beginning was a question of honour.—ANDRÉ SIEGFRIED.[1]

Forced upon the first French Company by the commanding influence of M. de Lesseps, a diplomatist and not an engineer, it entailed financial ruin upon his associates.—HENRY L. ABBOT, Brigadier General, United States Army, Retired, Formerly Member Comité Technique.[2]

ORGANIZING FOR WORK ON THE ISTHMUS

The first French construction group arrived at Colón on January 29, 1881, on the "Lafayette," in a party of forty engineers and officials led by Armand Réclus, an Agent Général of the Panama Canal Company. Five of them brought their wives to the Isthmus—the land so widely advertised in France as the "healthiest region in the world." Luxuriant in vegetation stimulated by the heavy rainfall, it was also subject to a most oppressive humidity, monotony, insects, and diseases and was as inhospitable to the unacclimated as it had been in the days of the railroad construction.

Although the Isthmus was crossed by rail, the land could claim only two cities, Colón and Panamá, the terminals of the railroad. The only other settlements were small groups of native huts near the railroad stations. Otherwise, the whole countryside, according to Lieutenant Charles C. Rogers, who had crossed the Isthmus in 1881 before excavation had been started, was a mass of "thickly matted jungle"[3]—a growth which could be penetrated only by means of a machete. Even today the jungle of the Isthmus presents essentially the same primeval appearance, except in those few spots where the land is kept cleared.

---

[1] Siegfried, *Suez and Panama*, p. 256.

[2] Abbot, *Problems of the Panama Canal*, p. 249.

[3] C. C. Rogers, Intelligence Report, p. 40 (U.S.).

This party under Réclus was probably the first real construction organization of the Panama Canal. It consisted of a Superior Agency, a Real-Estate Department, a Sanitary Service, and a Work and Construction Division.[4] The tasks facing Réclus were: to mark the exact location of the canal line, to clear the line of timber and jungle, and to open the country for excavation—all essential preparatory work which he expected to complete in about a year, using a system of direct employment of labor which was continued until Jules Dingler took charge in 1883.

It was De Lesseps' plan to start work with the large contractors, Couvreux and Hersent, who had agreed on March 12, 1881, to undertake and complete the work for 512,000,000 francs. But that contract was conditional; it was not to become binding until after two years.

The contractors sent their director, Gaston Blanchet, to the Isthmus to make preliminary plans. Rumors indicated that relations among the high officials were not harmonious, and within a short time Blanchet returned to Europe. To end these rumors of discord and dissension, on April 5 Réclus addressed a circular to all chiefs of brigades, letting them know that Blanchet had left for a short visit to Paris to settle the "definite order and course"[5] of the canal works and to advise about the manner of sending machinery and material to Panamá.

Gradually work took shape. "Leveling and surveying" were finished, and the line of the canal was more accurately determined. Activity started in construction of buildings and of dwellings for the laborers. A large frame house imported from New York was erected near Gatun, a sawmill was built at Colón, twenty small houses received from New Orleans were erected and partly occupied at other places, and twenty more from France and fifty from New Orleans were under order. In Europe and North America machinery was being manufactured,

---

[4] *Panama Star and Herald,* Feb. 1, 1881.
[5] *Ibid.,* April 8, 1881.

and by October deliveries were expected for excavators, flatcars, rails, dredges, hoisting apparatus, steam launches, telegraph materials, and even telephones.[6]

Besides planning for construction, another real obstacle of governmental nature faced the Canal Company when it learned that the Government of Colombia in 1867 had modified the railroad concession so as to give the railroad company a monopoly of transportation—canal, road, or rail. But the Government had reserved the right to grant a canal concession, subject to an indemnity to be paid by the canal to the railroad and to be shared with the Government.

De Lesseps from the beginning realized the necessity of controlling the railroad as an adjunct to his work. But from the first there was difficulty with the railroad, characterized by repeated delays of shipments, until arrangements for obtaining control of the road got under way in June. Faced with this difficult situation, he had no choice but to buy a controlling interest in the railroad's capital stock of 70,000 shares of $100 par value, at whatever price was demanded.

Not until August 1881 did the French gain that control. But at what a price—$17,133,500 for 68,534 shares at $250 per share, $7,000,000 for the company's bonds, and a bonus of $1,102,000 to the directors![7] Totaling over $25,000,000, or about one-third the resources of the Canal Company, it represented what André Siegfried called a "real Stock Exchange holdup." This arrangement, however, gave the French the necessary influence over the railroad company, while permitting retention of its status as a New York corporation—an effective gesture to public feeling in the United States.

In Paris the canal work was of another kind. De Lesseps had to keep up promotion campaigns with all his skill and optimism and at the same time run the Suez Canal. In his enthusiasm he was quoted as saying that the Panama Canal would

[6] *Ibid.*, July 29, 1881.
[7] J. B. Bishop, *The Panama Gateway*, pp. 53, 79.

be completed in six years, at another time in four years, although the period planned for the contract was eight years. In Panamá the press was critical of this exuberance in Paris; it wanted bigger salaries and more power to local officials. Before long reports were received in Panamá that the stockholders were kept informed by "watchers" and were dissatisfied with the way things on the Isthmus were being handled. But De Lesseps always had Suez to fall back upon; he reported an increase of 40 per cent in traffic during the past year and a remarkable net profit of 12,979,000 francs, or 21 per cent, and that he was preparing to light the Suez Canal with electricity to permit night transits.[8]

EARLY OPERATIONS IN 1881 AND 1882

Working forces increased monthly, with activity; but arrival of the unacclimated was followed by mounting illnesses. The first death from yellow fever among the 1,039 employees occurred in June 1881.[9] Later, the deaths from malaria exceeded those from yellow fever.

By fall materials had arrived via steamer in such volume as to fill the Colón storehouses, which at the time covered an area of 1,400 square meters. These arrivals included such large material as locomotives, cars, cranes, barges, and dredges.

Men could not be obtained as fast as required for the equipment, and it was proposed to import French convicts from New Caledonia. But local resentment against forced labor caused the idea to be discarded.

At first the offices of the company were located in separate buildings in Panamá. Consolidation under one roof was decided upon, to enable better enforcement of hygienic laws. The Grand Hotel on Cathedral Plaza, built during the years 1874 and 1875, was purchased and in December 1881 became the headquarters of the company. Upon the front of the building was placed a large sign "Compagnie Universelle du Canal Interocéa-

[8] *Panama Star and Herald*, July 5, 1881.

[9] I.C.C., *Number of Employees and Deaths from Various Diseases among the Employees of the French Canal Companies*, pp. 19, 24–37 (U.S.).

nique." Today this same building is the Panamá Post Office; but few of its callers realize that this building was once the French headquarters, nor do they know that it was the scene of historic festivities at the inauguration of the Panama Canal.

The year 1882 witnessed a variety of activities. First was a strike of canal and railroad workers on the Pacific side. Agitated by "Friends of Labor," the men demanded $1.50 per day, which they probably got in that day of rising wages and rising prices.

Next came the start of real excavation in Culebra Cut, which began formally in the Empire section on January 20, 1882,[10] and was celebrated by a banquet and ball in Panamá. This beginning was followed by the starting of excavations in the same year at Culebra, Mindi, Monkey Hill, Bas Obispo, Gorgona, Cristóbal, and Paraiso. But the dry season of 1882 was allowed to pass with little accomplished. Although excavators were available for use, there were no tracks arranged to carry either the excavators or their spoil. These ominous delays were the cause of general disappointment. Couvreux and Hersent continued with their surveys and preliminary work, but people became skeptical of what their machines could do on the Panamá Isthmus, which was alleged to be a "different affair altogether from the sands of Suez."[11]

While people were so anxiously waiting for serious work to start, all available space in Colón was covered with machinery in "glorious confusion," together with rails and ties for excavator tracks. But a great boom was expected in March, when between 3,000 and 4,000 men were due to arrive.

There were also events of civic importance in 1882. The first was the importation by the Canal Company of the first steam fire engines. Another was the adoption by the *Panama Star and Herald* of editions in three languages. The first issue, containing French, Spanish, and English, appeared on March 10, 1882;

---

[10] *Canal Record*, July 14, 1909, II, 362 (U.S.).

[11] *Panama Star and Herald*, Feb. 23, 1882.

the practice continued for over twenty-two years, extending into the period of United States occupation.

Engineers continued investigations of the Gamboa Dam and the Pacific terminal, and reports were sent to Paris. At the stockholders' meeting there on July 1 it was announced that the exact canal course had been decided, that the canal was a "private and commercial" enterprise, and that the first announcement date of completion was a certainty.

In New York an office of the American Committee of the Panama Canal Company was opened for the sale of canal securities under the direction of ex-Secretary of the Navy Richard W. Thompson. But his venture was not successful enough to help the French, who continued to be dependent upon private subscriptions in France.

In San Francisco the two brothers, Moses A. and Henry B. Slaven, and Prosper Herne became interested in the French canal work at Panamá. The elder brother, M. A. Slaven, was a mechanical engineer; the younger, a druggist. Desiring to benefit from the large contracts which they knew would be awarded, they bid $2,000,000 on a 6,000,000–cubic-meter contract, which was accepted about January 1882. With only meager resources, they interested capital in their project, formed the American Contracting and Dredging Company with offices in New York under H. B. Slaven, constructed a dredging fleet, and moved it to Colón with expectations of starting work in November.[12]

Meanwhile the Canal Company established a medical corps. Sisters of St. Vincent de Paul arrived from France to nurse the ill, and plans were rushed for hospitals. At Colón a 200-bed hospital was completed in March 1882. It was located on brick pillars extending out into the sea on the northern shore line, where it received the full force of the cooling breezes from the Caribbean. At Panamá the elaborate Ancon Hospital was started

---

[12] Robinson, *Panama: A Personal Record of Forty-six Years, 1861–1907,* pp. 150–58.

on the northeastern slope of Ancon Hill. The plant included an admission building, ward buildings, canteen, dispensary, servants' hall, kitchen, and residence of the Sisters. For its privileges the Sisters were authorized to charge each patient five francs per day. Dedicated on September 17, 1882, the direction of the hospital was given to Bishop Paúl of Panamá. Both vegetable and flower gardens, with many varieties of flowers, were set out under the direction of Sœur Marie Rouleau, Mother Superior of the Sisters of St. Vincent de Paul.[13] To protect the flowers from ants, waterways were built around the beds, and these became efficient breeding places for mosquitoes close to the unscreened windows of the hospital. Many of the patients thus became victims of mosquito-borne diseases.[14]

The hospital system was not complete, however, until a place could be obtained for convalescents to recuperate. This was found on Taboga Island, where the climate is drier and more bracing than at Panamá. Here the Hotel Aspinwall was purchased by the French Company and converted into the Taboga Sanatorium about 1885.

On the Isthmus preparatory work continued, and near the end of 1882 all arrangements for cutting of the canal had been made. Many houses had been built for laborers, great numbers of borings completed, several sections of railroad constructed near the work, and soundings had been taken in the sea near the future canal terminals. More than half the canal route had been cleared of jungle growth and the canal axis marked by stakes.

A contract was awarded the American Contracting and Dredging Company of New York to dredge the channel on the Pacific side toward the cordillera. The difficult central zone through the highlands was divided into small sections so that the contractor on each section could become expert in the problems of his particular terrain.

13 *Canal Record*, Aug. 3, 1910, III, 390 (U.S.).

14 L. T. Hess, "Ancon Hospital," *Surgery, Gynecology, and Obstetrics* (October 1920), XXXI, 424–29.

Most important, however, was the greatly increased understanding of the problems gained by the engineers, in spite of the
many loose statements that had continued to be issued since the
early promotion days. These promotional statements had been
so exaggerated and flippant that people in the United States, who
had been waiting a year to see work start, began to look upon
the canal project with "doubt and distrust." The early publicity
campaigns were accepted as necessary in the formative stages
of the promotion, but there was an increasing demand for reliable and definite information. It was hoped that with an increase of understanding by the engineers there would be better
dissemination of information and a corresponding reduction of
the political and financial opposition as the work proceeded, thus
leaving the veteran De Lesseps free to carry on his great work
unimpeded.

But this was not to be. Powerful interests in the United States
continued working against the French Company. De Lesseps
was compelled to stay in France to campaign for money in the
December 1882 drive and had no opportunity to follow the
project through personally on the Isthmus. This absence of the
leader was perhaps one of the greatest causes of the many difficulties and mistakes which the French Company experienced.

Admiral George H. Cooper of the United States Navy on
March 2, 1883, reported that the undertaking was so gigantic
that it could not be finished quickly; that the French were in
earnest; and that even if they should fail for want of funds, the
work accomplished would be so well done as to give the Panamá
route a great advantage over any other. Completing the canal he
considered as only a "question of money, for the undertaking
offers no insuperable engineering difficulties"; but the enormous
cost would deter investors from sinking money in an enterprise
from which any return would take so long. To its great promoter
he paid the compliment of stating that, even if this attempt failed
and another attempt should succeed at Panamá, credit for the
"design of the enterprise and of its energetic commencement"

would always be accorded to the French and especially to Ferdinand de Lesseps.[15]

With everyone thus expectantly waiting for work to start, a great blow came. The chief engineer of the contractors, Gaston Blanchet, died on the Isthmus. His company, Couvreux and Hersent, had rendered great service at Suez, but they did not know Panamá. They had not realized the debilitating influence of the climate upon Europeans, the prevalence of tropical diseases, the conditions of labor, the difficult terrain to be cut, and the great problems of supplying such extended activities in an undeveloped country so utterly lacking in productive enterprise. This large contracting company decided to withdraw from the undertaking, and on December 31, 1882, wrote to De Lesseps requesting cancellation of their contract. However, they offered to undertake the construction program on the basis of prices as determined by the preliminary work, but invited attention to the fact that these would be "onerous,"[16] as they would include the costs of mistakes, "groping in the dark," and the difficult conditions of labor and work in Panamá. Also they informed De Lesseps that they had found the system of awarding small contracts was the better. With the contractors off the Isthmus and with Blanchet dead, conditions went into a disheartening confusion. With no leader there was no program. De Lesseps had no other recourse than to accept the cancellation, and, with the assistance of his son, Charles A. de Lesseps, he proceeded to "rally the troops and to reorganize the army"[17] to carry on the struggle.

De Lesseps acted quickly by appointing Jules Dingler as Director General. He was an engineer of outstanding ability and splendid reputation and had served as Chief of Bridges and Roads in France. When his friends protested to him about going to work in the unwholesome climate of Panamá he scoffed at

[15] G. H. Cooper, *Progress of Work on Panama Ship-Canal*, p. 4 (U.S.).

[16] I.C.C., *Report, 1899–1901*, II, 12 (U.S.).

[17] Bunau-Varilla, *Panama: The Creation, Destruction, and Resurrection*, p. 32.

their words: "I am going to show them that only drunkards and the dissipated take the yellow fever and die there."[18]

Accompanied by his family and Charles de Lesseps, he sailed for Colón, arriving March 1, 1883. The first task was a round of Isthmian receptions. At the Grand Hotel, where the Company's offices were then located, there was a great arrival banquet with all the local celebrities present. Charles de Lesseps returned the courtesy with another at the same place. In his address he reflected the optimism of his father. He stated that there was much of which to boast—the different sections were installed, work was progressing on all sides, and within a year powerful machines would be competing. He assured them that his father would come again to watch the progress. The high light came when he told his guests they would be invited to witness the passage of the "world's commerce through the Canal"[19]—a view that was held by Ferdinand de Lesseps until 1885.

Dingler devoted himself to bringing order out of chaos. He restored discipline in the organization but in doing so incurred the dislike of those disciplined, who thereupon started rumors of extravagance. He organized work yards, studied the entire canal project, and submitted a voluminous report on the sea-level canal which was approved by the Superior Advisory Commission. He ordered machinery in quantity sufficient to undertake the work. Dingler's influence, as described by Bunau-Varilla, was "bold, loyal, scientific, and stimulating." He adopted the system of small contracts, of which nearly thirty were granted; for these the Canal Company rented the necessary equipment at low rates. The system had its difficulties—very frequent payments, many inspections to be made, and numerous suits before the Colombian courts.[20] But he got results, even in the early years when much of the excavation was done by

18 W. C. Haskins, *Canal Zone Pilot*, p. 194.
19 *Panama Star and Herald*, March 21, 1883.
20 Abbot, *Problems of the Panama Canal*, p. 40.

hand and removed by Decauville handcars well suited to the low grade of labor available.

Dingler's plan of the canal is interesting for comparison with other plans. All the French plans used the metric system, the line of the canal from Colón to the Pacific terminal being 74 kilometers. Originating in Limon Bay, it followed the valley of the Chagres about 45 kilometers to its Obispo branch. There it turned away from the Chagres and followed the Obispo toward the summit, which it crossed in a saddle 333.5 feet high between what are now called Contractors Hill (410 feet) and Gold Hill (540 feet). It then followed the Rio Grande valley to the Pacific. The bottom width of the canal was to be 22 meters (72 feet) and depth 9 meters (29.5 feet). The floods of the Chagres were to be controlled by a dam at Gamboa and by lateral diversions. The total excavation on the canal was estimated at 120,-000,000 cubic meters (approximately 157,000,000 cubic yards) —or 45,000,000 more than estimated by the International Technical Commission in 1880.[21]

Dingler attacked the highest peaks of the central region in April with 3 excavators, 7 locomotives, 70 cars, and a force of 400 men in Culebra Cut. Work was prosecuted vigorously. Before long there was much apprehension about slides and what bank slope to adopt to prevent them. It was expected then to have Culebra Cut finished by May 1885.

In the high central portion the work consisted of dry excavation. At Colón and Panamá, dredging fleets were slowly starting their way toward the center. French, Belgian, and American machinery was working in friendly competition, while a great mass of discarded machinery in confused disarray presented an effective monument to the mistakes of the first two years. This was the picture at the beginning of construction, called the "engineers' period"—a period supposed to last six years, until scheduled completion of the canal in 1888. The key to the future rested chiefly upon the problem of Culebra Cut.

[21] I.C.C., Report, 1899–1901, II, 15 (U.S.).

In Paris, Ferdinand de Lesseps, carrying on his distant campaign, did not weaken, and at a meeting of the stockholders on
July 17, 1883, he reaffirmed his belief in the 1888 completion
date and announced that the prejudices in the United States
against his plan had been dissipated. He said that the "sentiment of equity" which prevails among North Americans caused
them to understand that the French builders of the canal had
"no object in view but the removal of a material obstacle to
beneficial intercourse."[22]

The working force increased rapidly by importation of labor,
chiefly from the West Indies; in September there were about
10,000 men employed, mostly Jamaicans, with the work in "fullest swing." It is not surprising that the next issue of the *Canal
Bulletin* announced that all the undecided projects recommended
by Dingler had been approved by the Superior Advisory Commission. This included provision for tidal locks at the Pacific
terminal.

Originally the promoters had in mind the idea of a single
sea-level canal known as the "Strait of Panama." But Dingler
observed that the tidal range on the Pacific was about twenty
feet, but on the Atlantic only one foot. He concluded that the
currents set up by the difference of levels of the two oceans during changes in tides would be too dangerous for safe navigation,
and proposed a tidal lock at the Panamá end to preserve the level
from Colón to Panamá, a plan he thought would save the excavating of 10,000,000 cubic meters. The locks were to be in three
sections, one for exit, one for entrance, and one for repair, with
dimensions 25 meters in width and 180 meters in length.

Another public subscription for 171,000,000 francs,[23] offered in October 1883, was successful. De Lesseps was overjoyed and in a circular expressed his gratification and thanks for
the assistance in cutting the Isthmus of Panamá, which he thought
would be an achievement destined "to realize all the promises

[22] *Panama Star and Herald*, Aug. 2, 1883.
[23] Wolfred Nelson, *Five Years at Panama*, p. 258.

of the Suez Canal." But with each new subscription, money was becoming more difficult to get.

Near the end of 1883 activity on the Isthmus was so much greater that transportation facilities at Colón were overtaxed. The harbor was described as full of steamers, ships, barks, brigs, and schooners. All were laden with every class of material for the canal—machinery, iron, wood, and coal. Dock space was insufficient in spite of the seven wharves at Colón, and ships had to wait in the crowded harbor for weeks before they could discharge. But this did not hinder progress. Contracts were signed for excavation and for laborers, the company providing materials for contractors and houses for labor. It was confidently expected that the canal would be completed in 1888. This prediction was based on the assumption that during the first four months of 1884, the dry months, excavation would exceed that of the previous two years.

TRAGEDIES AND DIFFICULTIES

The year 1884 started off with a succession of difficulties and tragedies. In January one of the Slaven dredges, the "Prosper Herne," was destroyed by fire only a few days after arriving on the Isthmus. This loss slowed down the dredging program, but H. B. Slaven telegraphed his builders in New York to send down the next dredge and ordered an additional dredge in replacement.

In the last of the same month death struck the family of the energetic Chief Engineer. His daughter, Louise Dingler, who had just entered Isthmian life under such brilliant circumstances, contracted yellow fever and after a brief illness died. The population of Panamá was profoundly touched by this untimely death of the young woman. The funeral ceremony in the Cathedral of Panamá, with Bishop José Telesforo Paul officiating, and the cortege to the cemetery left a picture that was indelibly written upon the memories of the entire community.

But that was not all. One month later the twenty-year-old

son of Jules Dingler, a picture of health and strength, showed signs of yellow fever. Three days later he was dead.[24] The Cathedral of Panamá was the place of another pathetic scene.

Nor was that all. The young fiancé of the daughter, who had come over with the family from France, also was taken ill with yellow fever and died. Dingler did not falter, but kept the work going. Bunau-Varilla, who later worked under Dingler, wrote thus: "These trials which might have shaken the reason of any man did not drive this hero one step out of the path of his duty to the task in hand."[25] It was not until early June that Dingler, with his wife, left for France, not so much for rest as to take up the Canal program for 1885.

Unfortunately for the French, the part played by mosquitoes in causing yellow fever was not discovered until many years later. Because of that, even though the French Company had an excellent medical service and large hospital facilities, they did not take the steps which would have prevented yellow fever and malaria—that is, the eradication of the stegomyia and the anopheles and the screening of houses.

The French did not learn that breeding grounds for mosquitoes must be eliminated. Water troughs in the hospital grounds and water pans placed under bed posts to keep off insects served as fertile breeding places dangerously near unsuspecting victims, so that often after arrival in the hospital patients would contract yellow fever.

The disease obtained a reputation for mystery and elusiveness beyond description and struck fear into many hearts. But in spite of all that, Lieutenant Raymond P. Rodgers, writing on January 27, 1884, reported that the climate thus far had not proved so fatal in most of the canal sections as expected, that employees appeared in fair health, and that Europeans suffered more than the laborers who were natives of the tropics.[26] Such

---

24 *Panama Star and Herald*, Feb. 25, 1884.

25 Bunau-Varilla, *Panama: The Creation, Destruction, and Resurrection*, p. 33.

26 R. P. Rodgers, *Progress of Work on Panama Ship-Canal*, p. 24 (U.S.).

flare-ups of yellow fever as occurred in the neighborhood of
Panamá usually followed new importations of unacclimated and
nonimmune northern labor.

Rumors began circulating regarding the financial condition
of the company. A United States naval officer, Lieutenant Robert
M. G. Brown, sent to the Secretary of the Navy a report dated
June 2, 1884, stating that the company was in serious financial
straits, with $60,000,000, representing about one-half the capi-
tal, already expended, exclusive of the $20,000,000 paid for
the Panama Railroad stock, and with half the estimated time
for completion already elapsed but only one-thirtieth of the
work accomplished, and that largely theoretical rather than prac-
ical. He concluded: "The completion of this Canal, according to
present plans, is very doubtful. It certainly will require much
more time and money than originally estimated."[27]

To this, De Lesseps replied that there was no ground for
thinking the canal would not be completed in 1888. The excavation of 700,000 cubic meters[28] in June 1884 marked a new
high of production, attributable to the work of Dingler. But
even so, De Lesseps had to start another campaign for money
in August and September, and it was successful. De Lesseps announced that he intended to visit the Isthmus again in 1885
and that the financial condition of the company was "so flourish-
ing" it would enable excavation with "energetic impulse."

Later the generally pessimistic conclusions of Lieutenant
Brown found another advocate in Captain Bedford Pim of the
British Navy, who had visited the Isthmus in October 1884 "to
set at rest conflicting reports . . . . as to the progress of the
Canal." On November 8 he submitted his conclusions to the
Secretary of the United States Navy as a "private and confi-
dential" communication. Using De Lesseps' own estimates for
Panama that had been based on the totally different Suez work,

[27] R. M. G. Brown, *Report Regarding Progress of Work on Panama Canal*
(MS). J. E. Nourse, *Maritime Canal of Suez*, p. 148 (U.S.).
[28] *Panama Star and Herald*, July 24 and July 26, 1884.

Pim figured that excavations alone would require at least fifteen years because of the nature of the soil, ranging from slimy alluvium to strata of boulders and hardest rock and all subject to alarming slides, and also because of the difficulty of keeping the necessary 10,000 men employed during the annual long rainy season, with the certainty of sickness and death among them.

He said that the people of France were beginning to open their eyes "at the non-fulfillment of the promises of their idol," De Lesseps. There was "no perfidious Albion in the person of Lord Palmerston," who had opposed De Lesseps at Suez; and the absence of the United States flag from the Isthmus removed that country also from a position convenient for blame. He concluded: "It appears that the physical obstacles are insurmountable while the financial difficulties are scarcely less, although it is not yet too late to build a canal with locks. . . . . Every credit, not to say praise, has been given to the gallant employees who have struggled manfully to carry out the wishes of their . . . . chief, Mons. de Lesseps."[29]

The French people did not know what blackmail and coercion was going on in Paris. They only knew their aim to complete the canal, to win for France the double honor of opening the two great canals, and to immortalize the name of De Lesseps.

BUNAU-VARILLA BECOMES CHIEF ENGINEER

It was in this year of 1884 that a man destined to play an important part in the history of the Panama Canal and also in the formation of the Republic of Panamá entered the service of the company as a young engineer. His name was Philippe Bunau-Varilla. Able and ambitious, young and energetic, he possessed the qualities of character that admirably fitted him for his tasks on the Panama Canal, where he was to gain the actual experience that made him such a formidable protagonist for Panamá in later struggles.

Leaving France on October 6, 1884, he went to Panamá in

[29] Bedford Pim, *Remarks on the Panama Canal,* October 1884.

company with Chief Engineer Jules Dingler and wife on their return voyage to the Isthmus. Young Bunau-Varilla considered his trip to the Isthmus and his association with the Panama Canal as the realization of a childhood dream, and spent his twenty-one days on the voyage under Dingler's careful and probably exacting instruction.

At this time the canal was divided into three major construction divisions. The first extended from Colón over the greater part of the Chagres valley. A second included the remaining part of the Chagres and the Obispo valleys up to the foot of the Culebra slope. The third included Culebra and the Pacific slope.

Upon arrival, Bunau-Varilla was assigned as division engineer in charge of the Culebra and Pacific slope division, just in time to step into the key problem of Culebra Cut and the dredging of the channel from the Pacific up the Rio Grande valley. The work at Culebra had not proceeded rapidly. During January 1884 only 60,000 cubic meters were excavated, with 25,000,000 remaining in a section of two kilometers. At this rate it would have required a long time to complete, particularly with the necessary slowing down during the wet season. But tracks had been prepared and dumps were ready near by.

When the New Year's celebration arrived, another tragedy struck. Mme Dingler died of yellow fever.[30] Dingler, though crushed again, went to his office the next day as usual and kept the work going. He remained at his post until June, when he returned to France for the last time, exhausted and alone, having given up all his loved ones for Panama. He never lived in the fine quarters erected for the Director General's residence on the southern slope of Ancon Hill overlooking the islands on the Pacific. These quarters were eventually called "La Folie Dingler" by detractors of the canal.

This left Maurice Hutin as Director General; but he also suffered attacks of fever and in September had to return to France for his health. Young Bunau-Varilla at the age of twenty-six

[30] Bunau-Varilla, *Panama: The Creation, Destruction, and Resurrection*, p. 38.

then became acting Director General of the greatest engineering project of the world. He launched into his duties with the enthusiasm of youth, describing himself as "pitiless for all moral shortcomings, and the sincere friend of those who were valiant and devoted."[31] He restored morale among the workers and endeavored to establish cordial relations with the admirals of the two United States forces that were observing the progress of work on both sides of the Isthmus.

Shortly after Bunau-Varilla took charge, a new French Consul General, François Sébastian La Vieille, arrived, in August 1885. When introduced to the youthful chief engineer he expressed his astonishment at seeing so young a person in a position of such vast responsibility. In reply, Bunau-Varilla exhibited his astonishment at the Consul General's suggestion, saying that he thought it a republican principle to "judge men only according to their intrinsic value," and forthwith invited La Vieille to inspect the canal works and decide for himself as to his qualifications.

Later there was a welcoming party for the diplomat to meet the Company's employees. He had just come from home and brought words of hope to calm the minds of the workers disturbed by the incessant rear attacks on the Panama Canal— attacks that so unfortunately had kept De Lesseps promoting while he should have been at the helm on the Isthmus. Addressing the group, he gave a stirring appeal in support of Bunau-Varilla. Touching on the Frenchman's patriotic sentiment, he said: "The Canal work is French, and French it shall remain! France has begun it and France will complete it!" Then, referring to the work of De Lesseps and the many hindrances placed in his way, he said that "envy and evil prepossessions" would "sink conquered and impotent, like nature itself, before the will of the great Frenchman."[32]

Equipment continued to arrive from faraway places. "Dredge

31 Bunau-Varilla, op. cit., p. 48.
32 Panama Star and Herald, Oct. 31, 1885.

No. 19," built by M. M. Loebnitz & Co. near Glasgow, completed
in October its voyage of eighty-eight days through the Straits of
Magellan. That was a long voyage for the crew of twenty men
to make in such a clumsy craft, which the Captain described as
behaving "remarkably well." The eighth Slaven dredge, "The
City of New York," arrived at Colón after a twenty-day trip
from New York.[33] Put to work in the jungle, these dredges presented an imposing sight as the powerful forces of science and
the relentless forces of nature competed for mastery.

In his effort to promote good will, Bunau-Varilla made a formal call upon Admiral McCauley and upon Commander Lull of
the U.S.S. "Hartford," taking along a map to show the exact
line and the state of the work. On November 9 he conducted a
party of visitors to the work at Bohío Soldado, among whom were
Consul General La Vieille, United States Consul Thomas Adamson, Commander Lull, and Bishop Bernardo A. Thiel of Costa
Rica. There he showed some of the most difficult work and explained that, contrary to rumors, the work was being carried on
rapidly.

Later this same group went to Culebra to witness the work of
digging the Cut. The mountain was decorated with Colombian,
French, and Dutch flags and with flowers, presenting a sight unusual for the jungle of central Panamá. They visited the workshops, saw some dynamiting, examined the Cut, and watched the
experimental loading of an excavator, of which forty more were
on order. Bunau-Varilla explained that he had to extract
20,000,000 cubic meters in a distance of two kilometers and that
the slowness of the preliminary work revealed the difficulties that
were ignored by those who had not experienced them. The party
left, convinced that the work not only was possible but would be
finished soon.

Bunau-Varilla laid plans to increase excavation in a program
to total 1,400,000 cubic yards a month by January 1886. Work
progressed all along the line. At Culebra, work on the Panamá

[33] *Ibid.*, Oct. 1 and Nov. 2, 1885.

side was mostly by Decauville handcars, as only two hand-filled trains carried spoil to the dumps; on the Colón side, five excavators were taking 300 cubic meters each a day but were delayed by lack of spoil trains. Switching arrangements made it necessary for excavators to wait while trains went to the dumps and returned. At Paraiso rains caused slides of whole hills. In one slide the entire bank was carried "almost intact across the Cut with the top surface unbroken, and with vegetation undisturbed."[34]

This point cannot be left without paying a tribute to all the French engineers who directed this early period, particularly the unfortunate Dingler, whom André Siegfried has praised so highly for his "driving force and organizing ability" in getting the vast project under way.

CONDITIONS AT THE END OF 1885

Rumors of financial difficulties had spread widely. De Lesseps was having increasing trouble in raising funds. In May 1885 he wrote to the French Government, requesting authority to issue lottery bonds—a procedure he had followed at Suez when that project was about to fail for lack of money. But the Government hesitated. It desired to wait until the canal was investigated before acting upon the request. Armand Rousseau, an eminent engineer, was selected to conduct the inquiry on the Isthmus—an event to involve more delay and to have other serious repercussions. His function as understood in Panamá had nothing to do with the financial prospects of the company but was simply to determine whether the work could be completed with new efforts.

Apparently these rumors of financial difficulties had stimulated United States interest in securing later information than that contained in the reports of 1883–84 by Admiral Cooper and Lieutenant R. P. Rodgers. Another United States naval officer,

[34] W. W. Kimball, *Special Intelligence Report on the Progress of the Work on the Panama Canal during the Year 1885*, pp. 17–18 (U.S.).

Lieutenant W. W. Kimball, visited the Isthmus in 1885 and called upon Bunau-Varilla. Received with exceptional courtesy, he was given access to maps, tables, and descriptions of projects and was encouraged to make a complete inspection of the line of the canal.

His general observations as reported January 20, 1886, are of interest. Much housing, mostly barracks for laborers, was under construction; considerable construction plant was on hand, but not enough nor of the right type. Dredges were too few. French bucket-chain excavating machines were too light and were stopped by stones. Too much work was being done by small Decauville handcars—good for clearing ground but not for removing spoil on work that had been under way for two years. Kimball could not understand the necessity for constructing an artificial harbor in the east side of Limon Bay. With his background of experience on board ship in the bay, he naturally thought a better harbor could have been made by enclosing the bay with exterior breakwaters.

As to labor, largely Negroes from Jamaica and other islands of the Antilles, there was a large turnover, attributable to many causes—desire to return home to spend savings, poor food and high prices, inadequate medical care, fear of political disturbances, desire to leave the Isthmus before becoming ill, and probably simple fatigue from the Isthmian monotony.

In 1885 it was not possible to estimate a date of completion, as a normal excavation rate had not been determined. The company had made serious and costly mistakes; but these were not irreparable, and funds were being expended with economy. The company had the "necessary brains and energy" but needed more funds. Kimball concluded that if De Lesseps could raise the funds the work would be so far advanced as to make its completion necessary.

There had been much illness, and many French had died of yellow fever during the year; but malaria was an even greater destroyer. Deaths from diseases were not considered of great importance in relation to the completion of the canal, for there were always others to take the places of the fallen. While on the scene of operations, Kimball expressed the same idea differently: "As for human life, that is always cheap."[35] Later studies by Colonel Gorgas confirmed this view.

Adequate funds as the basic factor in assuring completion of the canal by the French Company is summed up by Lieutenant C. C. Rogers in his report of March 30, 1887, p. 57: "From all sources, whether friend or enemy, there comes the same admission concerning the great enterprise—that the canal presents no insuperable obstacles, and that its final completion is merely a question of time and money."

The time had come when De Lesseps would have to stage another spectacular act to attract attention. In Paris he publicly announced another voyage to the Isthmus to inaugurate the "period of final excavation of the Maritime Canal."[36] He stated that because the entire line was under construction with twenty-seven contractors under fixed-term contracts it was important that there should no longer exist any doubt concerning completion, so as not to discourage shipping interests from taking prompt advantage of the opening. He also said that, besides the French Chamber of Commerce, delegations from England, Holland, the United States, and Germany would accompany him on the visit.

The years 1883 to 1885 had been a period in which small contractors had operated under Dingler's aggressive leadership. Expenditures in the earlier years had been limited, but under Dingler's active schedule they mounted rapidly, making it necessary to seek funds continuously. But conditions in France in 1885 were not conducive to ordinary public financing because of heavy losses sustained by French investors in a stock-market crash. Small investors could not be interested. Furthermore, the delay of the Government in acting upon De Lesseps' request had made matters embarrassing.

[35] W. W. Kimball, *op. cit.*, p. 32.
[36] *Panama Star and Herald*, Feb. 13, 1886.

On the Isthmus, Culebra Cut had proved to be the almost insurmountable obstacle. In the dry season progress would be
made, but when the rains came "the dumps began to slide, the
tracks were cut, and general subsiding of the ground inside the
Cut paralyzed any movement of trains, and often overthrew the
excavating machines."[37] The large Anglo-Dutch contractors had
worked for a year and a half and had failed. One Dutch contractor had let so many subcontracts in the western hill at the
saddle that it became known as Contractors Hill. It looked as if
the canal would be completed everywhere along the line but fail
in Culebra Cut—a one-mile section through the main saddle
which seemed to overpower all efforts. Bunau-Varilla considered
it was "the life, the whole life, of the Canal which was to be
staked on this one card: the successful excavation of Culebra."[38]

In the effort to obtain money, advantage was taken of every
practical scheme. Gold was reported discovered in Cerro Culebra. The reputed discovery was publicized in the *Bulletin,* and
Cerro Culebra became known as Gold Hill. Much gold was
poured into that hill, but none was taken out. Indeed, the Culebra
Cut became a "bottomless pit into which money could be poured
forever."[39] This was reflected in the market price of the company's securities and forced consideration of less expensive
plans for crossing the Isthmus.

The engineers knew the only solution was a high-level canal,
to reduce the enormous quantity of excavation as well as to prevent slides. But Ferdinand de Lesseps, obsessed with his earlier
canal lessons, had to be convinced. He tenaciously clung to the
idea of another sea-level canal, as at Suez, and was unalterably
opposed to the idea of a permanent lock canal, although as late
as July 1885, after several years of work, only about one-tenth
of the estimated total of 120,000,000 cubic meters had been excavated. However, work had advanced enough to permit use of

[37] Bunau-Varilla, *Panama: The Creation, Destruction, and Resurrection,* p. 67.
[38] *Ibid.,* p. 68.
[39] Siegfried, *Suez and Panama,* p. 261.

locomotives and excavators by the last of the year. Use of hand labor by small contractors then was definitely out of order, and contracts were awarded to large companies which could work rapidly. Something had to be done to reduce the excavation to limits within the capacity of the Canal Company to pay and permit its completion within a reasonable time.

It was necessary for De Lesseps to visit the Isthmus a second time to dramatize the great work and to offset any injurious report which the Government Commission might make. Averring that the Panama Canal was far easier to construct than Suez, he reiterated his plan to complete it at the end of 1888. But valuable time had passed without making progress proportional to the time and expenditures. Almost six years had elapsed since De Lesseps had formally·inaugurated the Panama Canal on January 1, 1880. And he was aging—then in his eighty-first year.

CHAPTER V

FROM SEA-LEVEL TO LOCK CANAL

Construct a lock canal first and transform it later into a sea-level canal, by dredging.—PHILIPPE BUNAU-VARILLA, Acting Director General, Panama Canal Company, 1885–86.[1]

DE LESSEPS' SECOND VISIT TO PANAMA

Two hundred persons were waiting on a railroad platform in London on January 27, 1886, to bid Ferdinand de Lesseps and his party farewell on his second voyage to Panamá. Amiable as always, he was generous in his farewells to his many friends. Standing by the window of his railway carriage, he was smiling and confident. All present were profoundly impressed at the sight of this brave old man setting forth to effect the second union of the oceans. It was impossible to shake his hand without being awed by "so unfaltering a determination."

The locomotive blew the departure signal. He turned to the cheering crowd and said: "I shall be back in 60 days. I cannot die before opening my second canal."[2] Traveling with him to Panamá were representatives of the Chambers of Commerce from Marseilles, Rouen, Bordeaux, and Saint-Nazaire and also an eminent engineer, Peschech, from Germany, and another from Holland.

Arriving at Colón on February 17, he was received by the expectant crowd as a visiting monarch rather than as the president of a great corporation. To the engineers of the Panama Canal he had become a legendary figure whose decisions were sacred; to the Isthmians he was to be the creator of their age-long dream of a canal; to the French Nation he was the Great Frenchman; and to the world he was the great genius who was expected to effect a second union of the oceans.

[1] Bunau-Varilla, *Panama: The Creation, Destruction, and Resurrection,* p. 48.
[2] *Panama Star and Herald,* Feb. 27, 1886.

His son, Charles de Lesseps, was nominally vice-president of the company but actually its managing head. He had arrived on the Isthmus earlier in February and was the first to board the ship and greet his illustrious father. The party was joined by three representatives from the United States: John Bigelow, of the New York Chamber of Commerce; Nathan Appleton, of the Boston Chamber; and Admiral James E. Jouett, Commander of the United States naval forces in the Atlantic. Representing the British were the Duke of Sutherland and Admiral W. C. Carpenter of the British Navy.

Ferdinand de Lesseps looked well after his long voyage and moved around like a young man in spite of his eighty years. Nevertheless, six years of struggle had brought about its changes; he had aged perceptibly.

Two young ladies, one representing Colombia and the other France, presented him with flowers, initiating another elaborately planned program for entertainment as well as inspection.

His inspection covered the entire line of the canal, starting with a trip to Cristobal. There he was greeted by one of his pioneers, Alfred Tronchin, in an address indicative of the deeply loyal and intensely patriotic feelings of his employees. To De Lesseps he said: "You are for us the venerated chief around whom we are all grouped ready at all times to sacrifice even our very lives to assure your trimphant success in your present great and glorious work." Then, to stress the confidence retained by the canal personnel in spite of all opposition from its "detractors and calumniators," he declared emphatically, amidst shouts of approval and cheers, that the canal would be finished. The old man, moved by this stirring appeal and its enthusiastic responses, replied that he was proud of the "courage, energy, and abnegation" shown on the Isthmus and appreciative of the sentiments so clearly demonstrated. "With hearts and minds like yours everything is possible," were his concluding words.

A luncheon followed, attended by all the prominent Isthmian families. Admiral Jouett's band supplied music. De Lesseps circulated through the group saying pleasant words to all, often remarking that neither money nor hands would be lacking, for he considered the canal "an accomplished fact."[3] Later in the day he took a stroll about the city at a gait remarkable for a man of his years.

At Panamá his reception was equally lavish. The city was decorated with flowers, arches, and placards acclaiming the Great Frenchman; and crowning all were a triumphal procession, fireworks, and another banquet replete with speeches. The chief speaker was the eloquent Pablo Arosemena, who prophesied to De Lesseps that "the day will come when from the summit of the overpowered Culebra, the flags of all nations will announce to the world that you have crowned your glorious work; and the two united oceans will proclaim your victory and your greatness."[4]

In his youth De Lesseps had been an accomplished rider, and on his inspection tours of the canal he was usually at the head of his party on horseback. A member of the party wrote: "I saw him escalade at a gallop an escarpment of Culebra amid a roar of enthusiastic hurrahs from blacks and whites, astounded by so much ardor and youthfulness."[5] When he visited Empire, an accident occurred to the locomotive of his special train and the party had to walk to the foot of a hill where mules were waiting. Mounting, he galloped away to address a group of workers. Bishop records that there was a tradition on the Isthmus that De Lesseps rode like an eastern monarch in a "flowing robe of gorgeous colors."

At Colón, De Lesseps dedicated the statue of Columbus on February 24, 1886, at the site he had selected on his first visit to the Isthmus. Within a few days, when he was ready to leave, Colón tendered him a farewell breakfast. This was followed by his farewell address at the Columbus statue, in which he expressed his appreciation of the efforts of his collaborators. He

---

[3] *Panama Star and Herald*, Feb. 27, 1886.
[4] *Ibid.*   [5] J. B. Bishop, *The Panama Gateway*, p. 83.

then departed, "bright, vigorous and genial,"[6] for France, to re-
sume the financial campaign that was necessary to keep the canal
work going. The engineers and workers left behind were inspired to greater efforts.

THE LOCK PLAN STARTS

The reports submitted by the French Chambers of Commerce
were favorable. That of Government Commissioner Rousseau
was more searching. His inspection report, distributed in June
1886, supported the canal project. He considered it possible to
cut the Isthmus and that the project had gone so far that abandonment would mean disaster to the investors and to French
prestige in all the Americas. He recommended that the French
Government use its "diplomatic and administrative powers" to
aid the enterprise. He stated that the names and records of the
men who were directing the work, its humanitarian character,
and the serious efforts already made and still being made to accomplish it were deserving of the "special good will"[7] of the
Government. He urged the Government to avoid placing obstacles in the way, but instead to extend all aid compatible with
its position. Apparently Rousseau questioned the possibility of
completing the approved program under private subscriptions.
He suggested simplifications designed to advance the probable
date of completion and asked if it would not be possible "to
modify and simplify"[8] the plan—a question which implied the
lock-canal idea.

Another report was made by Jacquet, who had been sent by
the Company. He recommended abandonment of the sea-level
project and the prosecution of a lock canal in spite of the well-
known views of De Lesseps. Still another report was submitted
by Léon Boyer, who had worked with Bunau-Varilla. He bluntly
declared a sea-level canal impossible within the limitations of
the estimates and time. If not a diplomat, he had been in-

---

[6] *Panama Star and Herald,* March 13, 1886.
[7] *Ibid.,* July 18, 1887.   [8] Bunau-Varilla, *op. cit.,* p. 84.

BOHIO LOCK EXCAVATION, 1887

CULEBRA CUT OPPOSITE GOLD HILL, 1895
Showing house used by Bunau-Varilla

Courtesy of The Panama Canal

fluenced by a diplomat. Boyer, not wishing to oppose De Lesseps
too strenuously, recommended the idea of Bunau-Varilla—construction of a temporary high-level canal, later gradually deep-
ening to sea level by dredging.[9]

Even with these reports De Lesseps would not be moved at the
time from his insistence on a sea-level canal, and the Government delayed consideration of his request for a lottery loan, the
committee in charge adjourning until fall.

De Lesseps was disappointed but not defeated. "They have
adjourned on me. I will not accept this postponement. True to
my part, when they try to stop me, I go on." He had many
thousands with him in that decision; but the result must have
been uncertain, for he circularized his stockholders, stating that
although six deputies were trying to prevent him from winning
a "victory in this peaceful work undertaken by France in the
Isthmus, we will overcome every obstacle yet. You will march
with me to a second victory by providing the 600 million francs
I need!"[10]

Acting quickly, De Lesseps withdrew his lottery request and
went to the stockholders at their meeting of July 29, 1886, when
he asked for authority to issue bonds. He reconsidered previous
public statements and admitted that estimates would reach the
cost predicted by the Paris Congress of 1879. On the basis of
Suez data and the monthly excavation in Panamá in 1885 of
658,000 cubic meters, he optimistically predicted for 1886 a
monthly average of 1,079,000 cubic meters, for 1887 of
2,000,000, and for 1888 of 3,000,000. Basing his estimates
upon these figures, he declared the canal would be completed in
June 1889. He said the heaviest expenses for the first years had
been for organization, installation, and transportation, but that
the necessary plant had now been obtained and that all expenditures henceforth would be merely for fuel and wages. He acknowledged, however, that the higher charges on loans "must

[9] I.C.C., *Report, 1899–1901*, II, 17–18 (U.S.).
[10] Siegfried, *Suez and Panama*, p. 265.

augment the cost of the canal." He added that an early meeting would be held by the Consulting Commission to consider "modifying the plan of construction."[11]

Unfortunately, a definite decision was not announced promptly, and investors were left in doubt and in ignorance of facts. Although he appealed for 600,000,000 francs, the 354,-000,000 francs ($70,000,000) actually subscribed was nevertheless a truly remarkable response by the investing public for an undertaking then under such violent attack and resting upon such a precarious foundation. The subscription represented a tremendous personal tribute to the man in whom the people had faith and who symbolized their desire to support the resurgence of a defeated France.

So large were the fees required by the officials and extortionists in France that the company received only 200,000,000 francs out of the issue—enough to provide only temporary relief. De Lesseps looked to the United States for assistance, crossing the Atlantic later in 1886 in a vain effort. As a result he had to prepare for another financial campaign the next year.

THE ISTHMUS IN 1886

While the campaign for funds was going on in France in 1886, activity on the Isthmus did not stop. Early in the year Léon Boyer arrived with Charles de Lesseps to assume the position of Director General, relieving Bunau-Varilla. Though still a young man, Boyer already had attained distinction by constructing a great bridge in France. Described as having a powerful mind, he was just the type needed to succeed Bunau-Varilla, and after a month's instruction under him, Boyer took charge.

Shortly afterward Bunau-Varilla, worn out by many months of hard work on the Isthmus, contracted the dreaded yellow fever. With careful nursing by his friends he recovered—an event commented upon editorially by the press, which considered him a valuable member of Panamá society, an invaluable offi-

[11] *Panama Star and Herald,* Aug. 12, 1886.

cial of the Canal Company, as well as a man possessing "elevated traits of character and sterling qualities."

Weakened by his severe illness, he was carried on board a steamer for New York. Boyer saw him off, with a farewell embrace so typical of the French; and his friend sailed away, leaving the new chief engineer fully on his own.

In a short time Boyer was in a controversy with M. Lillaz, a member of the firm of Baratoux, Letellier, et Lillaz then working on the canal and the only member willing to direct the company's work on the Isthmus. The firm had a contract for dredging in the Rio Grande and Pacific entrance. One of its dredges sank, and Lillaz claimed reimbursement. He had already suffered some misfortune and resented Boyer's insistence that the contract prices covered all such unexpected losses. While nervously upset, Lillaz was taken ill with yellow fever. In delirium he summoned Boyer for an appearance with him before the "Supreme Judge within eight days" and shortly after died. For some reason there was a delay in the church service. The funeral cortege did not reach the cemetery until after dark, and the mourners had to stumble over tombstones as they walked to the grave.

Boyer, who attended the funeral of this contractor he had respected so much, was overcome with distress. Chilled by the dampness of the evening, the next day he too showed signs of yellow fever. Boyer had studied the problem of building the canal in detail and knew that the great struggle of the French was of critical importance. As he lay dying, his thoughts were of the great enterprise of which he was the leader and of the fear that it would be discontinued. His last words were: "Do not give up Panama."[12] Jacquet succeeded him.

Work kept on, with excavation records exceeding the performance in the same month of previous years. On January 1, 1886, the total of excavation from the beginning was nearly 18,500,000 cubic meters. For the entire year 1886 the total was about 11,700,000 cubic meters—a quantity equal to about two-thirds

[12] Bunau-Varilla, *Panama: The Creation, Destruction, and Resurrection*, p. 66.

the entire previous canal excavation record and almost approaching the prediction of 12,000,000 cubic meters for 1886 that De Lesseps had made in 1885[13]—an omen of success.

However, life had its gay side as well as dark, its sense of art and music as well as of industry. In December word came of the early arrival of Sarah Bernhardt, the noted French actress, after a triumphal tour of South America. Panamá, having had for several years a French-language section in the *Star and Herald,* had become quite cosmopolitan and was in the right mood for her visit. Her ship arrived December 28, 1886, just in time to permit changing dresses for the inaugural performance in a new theater filled to capacity by her admirers.[14] In response to popular appeal the performance was repeated the next evening. Then she departed, and the Isthmus reverted to its normal routine of work.

The year 1886 was marked by a large increase in the plant of the Canal Company on the Isthmus. The place now afforded a contrast to the unpopulated and impassable jungle of 1881. A United States naval officer, Lieutenant C. C. Rogers, who visited the Isthmus about this time, wrote that the canal and railroad appeared to lie in a "populous and prosperous" area. From Matachin to Culebra—the district of heaviest excavation—the region appeared as "one continuous settlement" instead of several stations on the railroad.

Also, the French had evolved a well-ordered permanent organization on the Isthmus under a Director General. There were eleven administrative divisions: Secretariat; Technical Bureaus; Accounts and Money; Material and Supplies; Workshops; Transport and Water Operations; and five Construction Divisions located at Colón, Gorgona, Empire, Culebra, and Panamá. There were 926 officials and clerks and 10,640 workers, mostly Jamaicans—too many officials for that number of employees.

To house canal activities, an amazing number of dwellings,

[13] C. C. Rogers, *Intelligence Report* . . . . *March 30, 1887,* p. 24 (U.S.).
[14] *Panama Star and Herald,* Dec. 30, 1886.

shops, and various kinds of buildings had been constructed, 1,131 being erected in 1886. As a rule, dwellings were located on hills along the line of the canal or railroad, so as to benefit from cool breezes. Rogers described them as of wood, clean, well ventilated and well suited to the hot climate of the Isthmus. Houses were rented to contractors by the Canal Company at 10 per cent of their value, and where workmen were quartered free they had to pay their own board at canteens kept as a rule by Chinese, who had gained the confidence of the blacks. Whites and blacks had separate quarters, and the offices and houses of officials and employees of the canal were "especially capacious and comfortable."[15]

ATTACKING THE GREATEST OBSTACLE

By the summer of 1886 work in the one-mile Culebra Cut had been progressing slowly for about four years, the last two under a large Anglo-Dutch company. Rains, slides, climate, sickness, transportation difficulties, and small equipment all joined with the laziness of workers to retard progress. The high peaks had been removed, but little else. In the four years the average altitude of the lowest points had been reduced by only 12 feet from the original 307 feet—that is, to 295 feet above the bottom of the 30-foot sea-level channel—a rate of only 3 feet a year. At that rate it would have required about 99 years to complete the trench between the oceans.

The Panama Canal Company officials became greatly perturbed. Bunau-Varilla, then recuperating in Paris from his illness and work on the Isthmus, suggested to Charles de Lesseps as managing head of the Canal Company that a special section of the Company be allowed to take over the Culebra Cut project under De Lesseps' direction, with full powers and freedom to select a group of men from the "best products of Isthmian selection," that is, those who had been tested and found qualified by actual work on the canal. While acting as Director General he

[15] Rogers, op. cit., pp. 39–40 (U.S.).

had brought the monthly total of excavation up from 720,000 cubic yards in January 1885 to 1,400,000 in January 1886 and felt confident of his ability to produce results. He was looking forward to resuming his position of leadership on the Isthmus and felt that, by remaining in the company's employ and solving the Culebra problem, he would be in a strong position to succeed as regular Director General. However, the Board of Directors did not approve of company operation for so important a task and desired to continue on the contract basis.

Thereupon, Charles de Lesseps proposed to Bunau-Varilla that he form a company to take over the work on the Culebra: "Why should you not put yourself at the head of a contracting company, the elements of which you would select according to your judgment? You would then be able to employ the full liberty of action which the strictness of the regulations of a great company like ours will never allow you. Act on the Panama Canal the part of Borel and Lavalley at Suez."[16]

Bunau-Varilla liked the idea of being a hero and accepted. His brother, Maurice Bunau-Varilla, took over the financial management. Two brilliant engineers, Artigue and Sonderegger, were the technical members, and Bunau-Varilla agreed to take over actual direction of the work at Culebra. The name "Artigue, Sonderegger et Cie." was adopted. The combination was certainly unique—technical knowledge, experience, youthful energy, and Bunau-Varilla's "passionate devotion to the Canal."

Resigning from the Panama Canal Company's service in September, he proceeded to Panamá. Within a short time he was living in a house on the side of Culebra Cut, watching the work proceed.

The Canal Company by then had succeeded in raising much of the money authorized in July, and the position of the contractors appeared more secure as work was rapidly resumed. The United States naval officer, Lieutenant W. W. Kimball, who inspected the Isthmus about the time Bunau-Varilla was starting

16 Bunau-Varilla, op. cit., p. 72.

his work at Culebra, stated that conditions on the canal were about the same as in January 1885, with one exception. That exception was Culebra Cut under Bunau-Varilla, of whom he wrote that since there was "plenty of capital behind him, great results may be expected from the efforts of a man of such marked and well-known ability, such energy, courage and perseverance."[17]

Work on Culebra Cut entered its most active stage during the French effort early in 1887, when 26 French excavators were digging and 42 locomotives were drawing 2,000 cars over a network of track, carrying the spoil to near-by dumps as it was excavated. Rogers wrote that the "Two thousand workmen engaged by hand, Decauville cars, excavators, and load-trains present a very animated scene."[18] But under the French regime the tracks of the Panama Railroad were not used for transporting excavated spoil to the dumps.[19]

With the "splendid plant" that the French then possessed, run by able contractors, Bunau-Varilla expected an increase in excavation despite the rainy season and the natural indolence of the laborers. There were, however, other great and unforeseen dangers in the path of progress.

When the rains came, the great mass of Cucuracha on the east bank south of Gold Hill began to creep slowly into the Cut at a rate of about 18 inches a year. The layers of clay, separated by mixtures of sand, alluvium, and conglomerate and made slippery by water saturation, moved as a result of the unbalancing of natural forces caused by the excavation. Bishop described the feeling of the French engineers as approaching consternation. They saw in the slides the end of the sea-level-canal dream. Excavation at Cucuracha was stopped, the slides came to rest, and the engineers undertook studies of the new problems which the advent of major slides presented.

Charles de Lesseps, with other company officials, arrived at

---

[17] Kimball, *Special Intelligence Report* . . . . *1885*, p. 32 (U.S.).
[18] Rogers, *op. cit.*, p. 33 (U.S.).
[19] Abbot, *Problems of the Panama Canal*, p. 41.

Colón from Paris in early March. He wanted to check the situation by a personal inspection and to arrange for future work with the contractors. Soon realizing the impossibility of completing the sea-level canal within the time limit, he admitted trouble in raising money for continuing the work and that its completion in time would require a revision of plans to a lock canal.

The solution of the Culebra problem then veered toward the lock-canal idea. Charles de Lesseps felt that two years of work would be saved by the reduction in excavation. The Director General, L. Jacquet, thought a lock might be placed at Culebra. But Ferdinand de Lesseps still had to be convinced, as he persisted in his views that locks were simply one of those "engineer's conceptions which had caused so much annoyance at Suez," where he had eliminated them by "letting nature and common sense take control."[20]

It was already too late. The company with its dwindling resources could not continue the sea-level plan, and only a high-level plan that would radically reduce excavation could save the day for the hard-pressed French Company.

Bunau-Varilla's earlier experience in dredging through the Mindi Hills provided the idea. He proposed to subdivide the central mass into a series of pools, place floating dredges in them, and then connect the pools by locks to make the waterway continuous. This would eliminate the problem of drainage caused by the tropical deluges and the resulting difficulties, such as detritus on rails and derailings, which had caused so much trouble to the French.[21] Also, by making the locks sufficiently large, it would be possible to conduct transits and to levy tolls while the work progressed. Such a lock canal was not to be considered permanent, but only as a transition period to permit the gradual digging of a sea-level canal. This concept of a "provisory lock canal" with a summit level of 170 feet met the objections of the old man, who reluctantly accepted. However, he

---

[20] Bunau-Varilla, *From Panama to Verdun*, p. 38.

[21] John Bigelow, *The Panama Canal and the Daughters of Danaus*, p. 16.

kept his ideal of a sea-level canal and still refused to accept the lock plan as the final solution, though announcing at a meeting of the stockholders in July 1887 that the company was seeking a new solution in opening a temporary canal without abandoning the sea-level plan.

Work at Culebra progressed rapidly while awaiting plans. During 1887 the average level was lowered 10 feet, instead of 3 feet as in the previous year. In 1888 it was lowered 20 feet, bringing the level to 235 feet when the works were stopped. On the basis of performance, Bunau-Varilla estimated that the level would be lowered 30 feet in 1889 and 50 feet in 1890, leaving 15 feet for lowering in 1891 to bring the level to the 140 feet required for a 30-foot depth with a summit level of 170 feet.[22] It appeared to him in 1888 as if this key problem were solved, that the excavation of Culebra Cut was within two and one-half years of completion, and that the canal would be open for traffic in 1891.

THE FINANCIAL CRISIS ARRIVES

What was happening in Paris during these critical months? Ferdinand de Lesseps realized the seriousness of the company's position. Pressure upon him came from all angles to alter the canal plans so that a waterway could be completed at reasonable cost and within the time limit. A meeting of his Superior Advisory Commission was called in January 1887 to consider the subject, and it promptly turned over the work of examining the several plans to a subcommission not due to meet until September. But no definite public announcement as to change of plans was made to prepare the public mind, in spite of the fact that all experts and even the commission headed by Charles de Lesseps recognized the impossibility of executing the company's program. Instead, the assertions of confidence in the sea-level canal continued, regardless of the ominous warnings of engineers. The public was kept propagandized to a view that was

[22] Bunau-Varilla, *Panama: The Creation, Destruction, and Resurrection,* pp. 73–74, 83.

104 AND THE MOUNTAINS WILL MOVE

without basis in fact. Perhaps a campaign of education as to real facts of the problem might have successfully maintained public confidence and prepared the way for raising additional funds certain to be requested.

The opposite was done. On January 18, 1887, De Lesseps wrote to the stockholders that he was convinced a sea-level canal was "realizable,"[23] as determined by the Paris Congress in 1879. He announced, however, that he had requested the Superior Advisory Commission to report on the lock plans already submitted and to examine other projects that would permit opening of the waterway with least delay but at the same time permit uninterrupted work toward the sea-level plan. In this last idea he probably referred to Bunau-Varilla's plan of a provisory lock canal as a logical step to permit construction of a sea-level canal later by dredging.

Canal circles in Paris were discouraged by the failure to raise funds in the United States. The directors vigorously opposed payment of the $25,000 annual bonus to ex–Secretary of the Navy R. W. Thompson for the use of his name. They wondered if it would not be better for the Canal Company to discontinue the American committee of bankers and depend upon France alone.[24]

There were other distractions, some humorous and some disconcerting. In Panamá a report on "Engineering Problems of the Isthmus" by a "teetotal liar" was reprinted. The report considered the difficulty of the Panama Canal as "two-fold, how to dam the water of the Chagres River and the flood of whisky at the same time."[25] He concluded that, had the cube of excavations "equalled the amount of liquor drunk along the line," the canal would have been half-finished.

The company had to face attacks not only from its natural critics but even from disloyal ex-employees. For example, on June 17, 1887, a cable from New York stated that J. Boulangé,

[23] *Panama Star and Herald*, Dec. 17, 1887.
[24] *Ibid.*, April 6, 1887.   [25] *Ibid.*, April 12, 1887.

an ex–chief of section at Bohío Soldado who had been discharged by Léon Boyer after a big fire in that section, had said in a speech before the American Society of Civil Engineers in New York that only 30,000,000 cubic meters out of a total of 140,-000,000 had been excavated, that the company had only enough money to last four months, and that he doubted De Lesseps could raise any more in France.[26]

Rumors about financial difficulties intensified, and, even by July 1887, reports of impending bankruptcy of the company were frequently mentioned. The development of slides, the failure to control the floods of the Chagres, and the increasing difficulty of raising money gave the rumors credence. Such a disaster would involve French national pride, affect her prestige among the nations, and ruin thousands of small investors—a condition of affairs certainly expected to force any French Ministry to aid the company.

A meeting of the stockholders was called and a new issue of bonds planned. The stockholders met in Paris on July 21, with the Emperor of Brazil in attendance. De Lesseps' report indicated a reduction in his confidence that the canal would be completed in 1889, but expressed the hope for a speedy joining of the oceans that would permit navigation pending completion. De Lesseps had come out for new plans belatedly and reluctantly. A misunderstanding arose because one of the plans provided for the definite substitution of a lock canal for the sea-level plan. To this De Lesseps replied: "I shall never consent to such a substitution." He said he would never depart from the plan of the Paris Congress of 1879, the "*sine qua non* of our enterprise."[27]

Financing required greater inducements to attract new investors. The new subscription for $100,000,000 announced for July 26, which was at a discount of 57½ per cent, gave a net return of only $42,500,000. With only $20,000,000 reported as left in the treasury, this small amount would not last long at the rate funds were then required on the Isthmus.

26 *Ibid.*, June 18, 1887.   27 *Ibid.*, Dec. 17, 1887.

In faraway San Francisco the situation was being watched. The *San Francisco Bulletin* commented that this bond issue "probably marks a crisis in the affairs of the Company." It further stated that, if the new loan were taken, it would indicate that "well-informed financiers discredit [Isthmian] rumors of . . . . insurmountable obstacles to the completion of the great work; and that the enterprise will be pushed to a finish." If it failed, the company was in danger. In any event the Panama Canal would go down as the greatest business promotion in the history of the world. To escape a real catastrophe, two solutions then seemed possible: France might take over the work, or a new company might be organized to take over at a small fraction of the original investment.[28]

First dispatches from Paris announced that the loan was subscribed in full, that there would be no delay or stopping of work, and that there was "unbounded faith" in De Lesseps. But that faith did not stop rumors, for in Panamá reports were rife that the loan was not subscribed in full; but nothing could stop the optimism for final success, despite the "idle rumor." When the final result was announced it showed that only two-thirds of the loan was subscribed, producing 114,000,000 francs, which De Lesseps considered sufficient to meet needs to carry on work for two more years.[29]

While the lock-canal project was being considered, De Lesseps on September 25 called another stockholders' meeting to obtain their opinion about the change of plan forced by circumstances. He reported that "incessant and bitter assaults" of adversaries, which did not frighten the shareholders, had succeeded in intimidating the financial world, making financing increasingly costly by the mounting annual fixed charges. He stated that everything to expedite work had been done and that nothing had been neglected "which would encourage, support, and assist"[30] those working with him. Some had measured up

28 *San Francisco Bulletin*, July 16, 1887.
29 *Panama Star and Herald*, Aug. 8, 1887.   30 *Ibid.*, Dec. 17, 1887.

to expectations with "courage and devotion," residing on their sections of the work. Others produced inferior results by obtaining inferior laborers, causing what he hoped were only temporary delays. It would require another $150,000,000 to open the canal, with 60 kilometers of the total 74 completed on time. The 14 kilometers through the cordillera, already deeply cut, would have to be closed to form a lake with locks at each end, to permit dredging to sea level at the same time as the canal was being used for transiting vessels across the Isthmus.

The Superior Advisory Commission, consisting of the most eminent engineers of France, submitted its report in October, stating that it was possible to establish a high-level canal through the central mass on the Isthmus so as to permit later dredging to sea level and that it would be possible to transit ships during the process. De Lesseps was then ready for his next move.

On November 15 he sent out two letters. One was to the French Minister of Finance, again requesting authority to issue 600,000,000 francs of lottery bonds to cover expenses from January 1, 1888, to inauguration about 1890. He briefly outlined the conditions facing the company, stating that latest plans left about 40,000,000 cubic meters to be excavated—10,000,000 rock and 30,000,000 dredgable.[31] To the shareholders, De Lesseps "the untiring," in another dramatic move, announced arrangements with Alexandre Gustave Eiffel, the builder of the Eiffel Tower, for construction of locks to open navigation. He referred to the attacks made on the company—false letters, false telegrams, false circulars and pamphlets, designed to cause the fall of canal securities on the Bourse and "to dispossess you of your property and of your titles on the eve of your efforts being crowned with success." He appealed for unity among both bondholders and shareholders. "Let them remain deaf to the advances of their intended defenders" and to the "menaces of their foes," for he would be the first to warn of danger to their great enterprise.[32] The French Government de-

[31] *Ibid.*, Dec. 14, 1887.   [32] *Ibid.*, Dec. 17, 1887.

layed, but De Lesseps displayed confidence with his business associates. When H. B. Slaven, who was with De Lesseps during this period, returned to New York he reflected the views of his chief, based upon six years' working on the Isthmus and not upon "observations made from car windows."[33] He reported the canal as more than half completed, that the Culebra was still the greatest problem, and that De Lesseps and Eiffel expected to visit Panamá in January. He expected the canal to be opened in January 1891, because machinery was available, the organization had been perfected, and men were becoming acclimated.

But De Lesseps could not make his trip to Panamá. He had to stay in Paris to raise more money when the French Parliament refused his request. Irked by this refusal, he announced he would appeal directly to the people. He declined to accept the Government's decision as to the lottery bonds, urged the shareholders to put pressure on representatives for a public inquiry, and called a meeting of the shareholders for March, while the shares on the Bourse continued their downward spiral.

In spite of these preoccupations he had time enough to travel, always in the interest of Panamá, and time to be interested in people. One day two salesmen found themselves in the same compartment with an old man whom they supposed to be of the same profession, and one of them started conversing with him:

"Beg your pardon, sir. What is your line?"

"Isthmuses."

"Wh-wh-what?" was the puzzled reply.

"I am introducing ship-canals."[34]

The old man was Ferdinand de Lesseps. He was certainly trying to sell canals, for while heading the great effort at Panamá he was still running Suez. But he also had another great vision which he was interested in promoting—the Kra Canal across the Malay Peninsula as the natural supplement of the Suez route to China—thus completing the canal route around the world.

[33] *Panama Star and Herald*, Dec. 13, 1887.   [34] *Ibid.*, Feb. 27, 1888.

CHAPTER VI

FRENCH MONEY RUNS OUT

He [Ferdinand de Lesseps] offered . . . . *the magnificent spectacle of an old age retaining to the full the energy and buoyancy of youth. No difficulties deter him, no obstacles, natural or financial, present themselves to his mind as too vast to be overcome.*—LONDON TIMES, September 7, 1888.[1]

WORK ON THE ISTHMUS IN 1887 AND 1888

When it became evident late in 1886 that the French plans would have to be changed, many contractors, fearing to risk expending too much effort on uncertain plans, slowed down their works and thereby delayed prospective completion until 1889. At Culebra Cut, however, all excavation was usable regardless of the type of canal, and work continued unabated.

How was the canal work organized to enable completion by 1889? Laid off in sections measured in kilometers, beginning at Colón, the canal was 74 kilometers long. For construction it was divided into five major construction divisions, each assigned to a large contractor. The first 25 kilometers from Limon Bay, following the valley of the Chagres to Bohío Soldado, were being excavated by the American Contracting and Dredging Company, controlled by the Slavens. The section from kilometer 26 to 44, which extended as far as Gamboa, was assigned to Vignaud, Barbaud, Blanleuil et Cie. The Public Works and Construction Company operated from kilometer 44 to 53.6, up the valley of the Obispo to the high Culebra Cut, and also worked on the dam for the Chagres at Gamboa. The highest part of the central mass then called Culebra Cut, between kilometers 53.6 and 56, was under Artigue, Sonderegger et Cie., the firm organized by Bunau-Varilla. Baratoux, Letellier et Cie. worked from Culebra Cut to the Pacific Ocean.[2]

[1] *London Times*, Sept. 7, 1888, p. 7.
[2] I.C.C., *Report, 1899–1901*, II, 16 (U.S.).

Although there was much uncertainty as to definite plans, work progressed in spite of periodic rumors of many discharges on the Isthmus, which always spread alarm. Excavations in April 1887 and again in August were over a million cubic meters each month. By the beginning of 1888 Bunau-Varilla estimated remaining excavation at 56,000,000 cubic yards, which an average annual quantity of 16,000,000 would complete in less than four years, permitting opening the waterway in December 1891.

Work continued on diversions as well as on the main canal, so as to keep the Cut free of water. Everyone was looking forward to diverting that turbulent river, known as "Father Chagres," into new channels to eliminate its recurrent ravages, which from the first had constituted a major problem for the French.

It was heartening to De Lesseps in Paris to receive word late in November 1887 from the engineer Nouailhac-Pioch[3] that he had steamed from kilometer 17.4 (near Lion Hill) to Limon Bay on the Atlantic, and that on the Pacific the mud scows were towed at low tide as far as kilometer 67.8, a point where today the Balboa inner harbor is located.

Work on the canal was not without its amusing incidents. The engineer of the Pacific division, Norge, after an inspection of the work at La Boca, had returned to Panamá City. There his mules became frightened and made a wild rush toward the Canal Office Building. In the dash through the gateway one of the wheels struck a post and was wrenched off, but the mules kept on going and would have run into the sea in a short time. Unfortunately for one of the mules, a sailor was waiting for a boat with an oar in hand. With a wide swing he struck the head of one mule with such force that the animal was felled forever. For this act he received the plaudits of the crowd, who in their exultant relief from Isthmian boredom took up a subscription for the valiant mariner.[4]

---

[3] *Panama Star and Herald*, Jan. 4, 1888.   [4] *Ibid.*, Nov. 1, 1887.

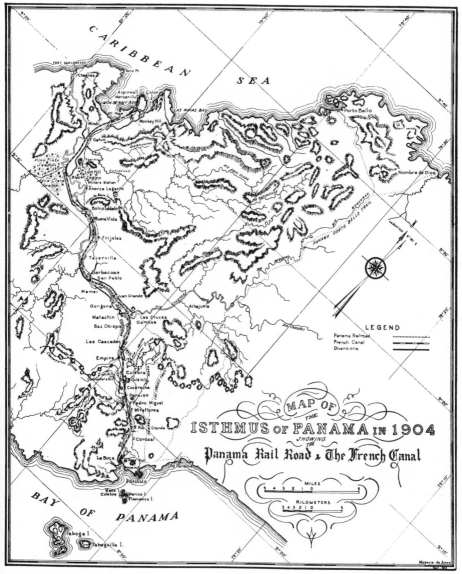

MAP OF THE PANAMA RAILROAD AND THE FRENCH CANAL, 1904
Drawn from records of The Panama Canal

From New York came more rumors about canal difficulties—
there was no work in progress, two leading contractors were em-
barrassed, judgments had been filed against the French Canal
Company with seizures and sales, and there was a too obvious
effort to "keep up the appearance of life."[5] Offsetting these attacks, the *Canal Bulletin* in December announced that ships were
landing cargoes directly to trains at the Pacific terminal, thus
avoiding the double handling previously necessary. On the
Atlantic end the canal was used to deliver supplies for work on
the Chagres.[6]

Work on the lock canal finally started at Pedro Miguel on
January 15, 1888, and at San Pablo in February. The same
general canal route was followed, with a summit level of 49
meters (170 feet). This placed the summit level above the flood
waters of the Chagres so high that it was necessary to feed the
summit level by machinery. There were to be ten locks, five on
each slope. On the Atlantic slope were Bohío Soldado, San
Pablo, Matachin, Bas Obispo, and Empire. On the Pacific side
were Cucuracha, Pedro Miguel, Miraflores, and a double flight
at La Boca. This was a small canal with a bottom width only a
fraction over 61 feet. All locks were to be located over compact
rock near railroad stations, and lock gates were to be manufactured in Europe by Eiffel, using a modified form of his plans for
a Nicaragua Canal.[7]

Meanwhile, Panamá witnessed another celebration. On
Washington's birthday in 1888 the stone barrier at Mindi Hill
was removed after five years of hard work. This meant that
the canal was open from Colón past Gatun to Bohío Soldado,
with sufficient depth for vessels of 1,000 tons. It was the occasion for a celebration, with a visit from celebrities who went by
steamer past Gatun.[8]

In May 5,000 men were working on ten lock sites. The

[5] *Ibid.*, Nov. 23, 1887.
[6] *Ibid.*, Feb. 4, 1888.   [7] *Ibid.*, May 18, 1888.
[8] *Ibid.*, Feb. 23 and Feb. 24, 1888.

Pedro Miguel site was reported as one-third completed, and five locks were expected to be ready in several months. Dredging continued with increased momentum. With ten new dredges due to arrive before the end of the year, excavation was expected to reach a monthly total of 1,500,000 cubic meters, with prediction of completion dates varying from 1890 to 1891.

One writer has left a vivid record of work at the San Pablo lock. Viewed from one end, he saw about 600 men working in the 270-by-18-meter lock space. "Here, boring the holes for the next blasting, are the 120 miners; here are men loading the large buckets which as soon as filled are lifted by the cranes up to the level of the top cut, some fifty or sixty feet, and emptied upon railroad tracks; and here on a higher cut are men who load the cars from the ground; at the ends of the locks are still other gangs with wheelbarrows wheeling the earth away to the dumps as fast as the barrows can be loaded."[9] Many kinds of machinery and labor-saving devices were near by—rock crushers to prepare rock for concrete, machine shops with lathes, bolt-cutters, punches, and saws, all steam-power operated, and a blacksmith shop with flaming forges. Work was pushed night and day.

At Paraiso and Miraflores were the same pictures of action. There winches were hauling "large and heavy trains of the Decauville dumping cars out of the work, up steep inclines," pumps were draining water from the sites, and the appearance presented was that of a "gigantic undertaking well-handled,"[10] with workers in good health.

Another tragedy struck the engineering staff when the new Director General, Antoine Vanneau, died on June 27, 1888. He had symbolized the speed and the energy of the French in trying to accomplish their belated plans and to protect the interests of the company and of France. Buried near his work, his own words were used for his epitaph: "However sad may be the mis-

---

[9] *Panama Star and Herald*, July 17, 1888.
[10] *Ibid.*, May 12, 1888.

fortunes which have befallen us in this climate, we must not lose confidence. Let us remember that we have given ourselves to a work which is very important and has become national, and, proud of engaging in it, I had almost said of fighting with it, for the glory of France; let us close our ranks and push on to the completion of the Canal in three years."[11] The death of another leader did not affect the work. There were always three more to replace each one who fell.

Sections of the canal were nearing completion; Culebra was advancing, and preliminary work on the Chagres Dam commenced. Relocation of the Panama Railroad was started so as to get it clear of Culebra Cut, the new location requiring a large bridge across the canal at Paraiso. At Matachin the head of the lock was almost ready to receive fittings. All lock sites were being excavated.

As the year 1888 closed, Culebra Cut work under Artigue, Sonderegger et Cie. showed remarkable progress. In July about 5,000,000 cubic meters remained to be excavated in that short but difficult section. Between 2,500 and 3,000 men were employed day and night in a cut lighted by electricity. With 800 dirt cars and 54 locomotives operating on 37 kilometers of track at a rate of 100 trains a day, these scenes of feverish activity were intensified by the 23 steam excavators that kept the trains supplied.[12]

At first the critics claimed the Cut structure was "too hard to be pierced." When the work appeared successful the form of attacks changed—it was "too soft." Then the theory of "sliding mountains" that would defy all efforts arose to cast its pall upon men's minds. But the work continued at Culebra and was vividly described as late as December 1888 by one who said that even to see the machinery in operation would take one's breath. "Enormously powerful dredges tear up the earth from the bed of the Cut and force it through seemingly impossible

11 *Ibid.*, June 28 and June 29, 1888.
12 *Ibid.*, July 26, 1888.

lengths of pipe to its destined resting place, whilst all along the sides of the Cut mighty excavators, moving slowly along the railroad tracks, tear away the bowels of the mountains with incredible rapidity, and deposit the debris in cars that bear it away . . . ."[13] It was expected that the Paraiso bridge would be ready in January and that the dredging of the actual channel in Culebra Cut would begin in March.

But in the midst of such promising activity there was a suppressed sense of danger. Disconcerting messages that had arrived from Paris were whispered around but not published. Only a few realized the gravity of the rumors, as the work was pushed onward with completion expected in 1891.

LAST EFFORTS OF DE LESSEPS TO KEEP GOING

While such great effort was being made in Panamá, what was happening in Paris? The shareholders' meeting, called by De Lesseps when the Government refused to authorize lottery bonds, met on February 29, 1888. More than a thousand attended, and Ferdinand de Lesseps presided. With excellent precision he read his report for forty minutes. The audience consisted chiefly of middle-class small investors to whom a collapse of Panama would be a personal disaster. De Lesseps, interrupted by frequent applause, gave a résumé of the situation— the necessity for more money, how the ill will of the opposition forced higher interest rates upon the company, and how the directors had been induced to adopt a temporary lock canal so that it could be opened in 1890 and completed later.

Charles de Lesseps followed with an appeal for confidence and advised the investors to hold their shares as the only way to safeguard their great enterprise. The shareholders then authorized a loan of 340,000,000 francs. It was estimated that the cost to complete would be 654,000,000 francs: 254,000,000 for excavating, 125,000,000 for locks and masonry, 15,000,000 for reservoirs and summit-level supply, 50,000,000 for mate-

13 *Panama Star and Herald*, Dec. 4, 1888.

rials, and 210,000,000 for general purposes. With the loan of 340,000,000 francs and the 260,000,000 already authorized, plus 110,000,000 on hand, there would be a margin of 56,000,-000 francs.[14]

At the same time the French Parliament reconsidered its previous action, and a bill authorizing issue of lottery bonds was introduced. It met determined hostility. Some opposed because they considered the company's estimates unreliable, others because they did not believe it a government function to guarantee a private company. Friends of the company in Parliament appealed for members not to abandon this national enterprise, and the lottery law was passed by the Chamber of Deputies on April 28 and by the Senate early in June 1888, after long debates in both Houses. On the ninth of June De Lesseps announced the terms of the issue, scheduled to take place on June 26.[15]

De Lesseps continued with his campaign, on one occasion speaking before the Topographical Society of France (Société de Topographie de France, Paris). Wearing the large ribbon of the Legion of Honor, he read an illustrated paper, renewing his assurance that the Panama Canal would be open in 1890. As proof he pointed to his photographs, saying, "The sun is our best collaborator, for he furnishes to photography the means of refuting the calumnies of our adversaries."[16] He then reverted to the familiar refrain that he would triumph at Panama as at Suez.

In Panamá the *Star and Herald* advertised the offering of 720,000,000 francs in bonds of a normal value of 400 francs, offered at 360 francs.

The Canal enemies did not wait till the day of issue. Three days before that date they dumped shares of the company on the market to depress the prices. Then, knowing how much the

[14] *Ibid.*, April 20, 1888.
[15] I.C.C., *Report, 1899–1901*, II, 20 (U.S.).
[16] *Panama Star and Herald*, June 27, 1888.

public pinned their hopes on De Lesseps himself, on the day of issue they telegraphed throughout France the false news of De Lesseps' death. Notwithstanding these insidious attacks, out of 2,000,000 bonds issued, 800,000 were subscribed by 350,000 persons. But this failure of the offering represented a great break in the company's credit and was quickly reflected in depressed security values. Bunau-Varilla thought De Lesseps should have been permitted to limit the issue to 660,000 bonds, as advised by Baron Jacques de Reinach; but this was not permitted by the bank, which insisted that all the 2,000,000 bonds be offered at one time. Bunau-Varilla considered this failure in financing the fundamental error that precipitated the collapse of the Old Panama Canal Company.[17]

In their desire to economize, the company did not cable the news to Panamá. Other lottery drawings were scheduled for October and November. To stimulate interest, De Lesseps and his son visited many industrial and commercial areas in a frantic and "laborious work of propagandism."[18] In their appeals they referred to the Loire factories in Nantes, where the lock parts were being constructed by Eiffel and where they had seen sizable parts 24 meters long, 3 meters thick, and 10 meters high, weighing 230 tons. They continued to speak in November but did not meet with their expected success, and hope was abandoned of disposing of all the remaining 1,200,000 unsold bonds.

In Panamá security prices trembled. The propaganda of De Lesseps' enemies was bearing fruits. On November 24 word came from London of the alarm felt by De Lesseps. He threatened "to publish an account of every step he had been forced to take in the Panama Crusade"[19]—steps that were supposed to involve several members of the Cabinet.

The November issue was not to be irrevocable unless 400,000 bonds were subscribed, but less than 200,000 had been sub-

[17] Bunau-Varilla, *Panama: The Creation, Destruction, and Resurrection*, pp. 87–88.

[18] *Panama Star and Herald*, Nov. 13, 1888.

[19] *Ibid.*, Nov. 26, 1888.

scribed. The French Government showed intense anxiety at the possible public reaction. Conferences were held between De Lesseps, the Directors of Credit, the Minister of Finance, leading jurists, financiers, and Senators. De Lesseps informed the Government of the facts. He wanted to promote a new company to continue the work. On December 14 a bill providing for a three-month moratorium on bills and for interest and securities was introduced in the Chamber of Deputies. The same day De Lesseps petitioned the Civil Court of the Seine to appoint temporary managers to take over, so as to prevent stoppage of work on the canal. Senator Denormandie, former Director of the Bank of France, Baudelot, ex-president of the Chamber of Commerce, and M. Hué were appointed. With them secured, De Lesseps cabled to Panamá his hopes of realizing such a combination[20] as to insure continued progress, and Denormandie sent authority to continue until February 15.

THE CULMINATION OF THE CRISIS

Another blow came just as De Lesseps had completed plans leading to the formation of a new company. The bill of the Government providing for three months' postponement by the company of payments on its bills and interest came up for a vote on December 15 and was rejected, 256 to 181, in the Chamber.[21] Ten minutes after the vote a reporter called on Ferdinand de Lesseps and told him about the rejection. Pale and speechless, his hand fell like a stone. Placing a handkerchief to his lips to stifle a cry, he said:

"C'est impossible. C'est indigne! I did not believe the French Chamber would sacrifice the interests of the Nation. They forget the milliard and a half of the savings of the French people that are compromised by this vote, and they could have saved all this by a firm decision. This will be a triumph for our enemies, and a disaster to our flag."[22]

---

[20] *Ibid.*, Dec. 17, 1888.   [21] Bunau-Varilla, *op. cit.*, p. 93.
[22] *Panama Star and Herald*, Dec. 19, 1888.

At the office of the company there were scenes of wildest confusion. The hall was crowded with subscribers. Women were weeping excitedly at the loss of their small savings, and men were facing ruin. All waited for Ferdinand de Lesseps to appear. Mounting a platform, he addressed them in an effort to restore confidence: "My friends! Your subscriptions are safe. Our adversaries are confounded, and we now have no need of financiers. You have saved yourself by your own exertions. The canal will be made!"[23] Cheers! Cheers! Cheers! De Lesseps wept at this powerful demonstration, as all hands closed in to shake his hand and women in tears tried to kiss his clothing.

The next day many came with more money. Some even brought their children's savings, but were disillusioned when they found that only by government aid could the canal be completed and that De Lesseps had withdrawn, leaving control to the temporary managers.

The Paris paper *Le Figaro* commented that the Chamber of Deputies had played into the hands of the North Americans. Friends of De Lesseps blamed the hostility of the United States and the lottery scheme for the debacle. But De Lesseps had asked successive public subscriptions of great sums, and probably the last was too much. He had been attacked at home.

From Washington came still another blow to those who hoped for assistance from the French Government. Senator Edmunds of Vermont introduced a Joint Resolution (Sen. Res. 122) on December 19, 1888, expressing "serious concern and disapproval" of any European government's connection with "the construction or control of any ship-canal across the Isthmus of Darien or across Central America." Declaring such connection or control as "injurious to the just rights and interests of the United States and as a menace to their welfare," the President was requested to "communicate this expression of the views of Congress to the governments of Europe."[24] In spite of all this

[23] *Panama Star and Herald*, Dec. 19, 1888.

[24] G. F. Edmunds, "Joint Resolution (Sen. Res. 122)," *Congressional Record*, Vol. XX, Pt. 1, p. 338 (U.S.).

opposition, a meeting of 4,000 bondholders passed a resolution of confidence in De Lesseps and expressed willingness to forego interest payments until the canal could be opened for traffic. These combined events created profound depression in France. In Panamá the message of De Lesseps to Director General Jacquet on December 15, about the appointment of provisional managers, had restored calm but not confidence. Isthmian shareholders, instead of throwing over their "Grand Old Man," sent him messages of trust and promises of support. The canal became the principal topic of conversation. The Panamá public concluded that the crisis had become a collapse. But contractors continued work to show their faith, and all were asked to withhold judgment. France rushed a warship toward the Isthmus in anticipation of disorders, and two were expected from the United States—a precaution laughed at by the Isthmians, who pointed to their tatterdemalion army of 600 ready to handle anything. Word came to Artigue and Sonderegger on January 7 to suspend work.[25] Twenty-five hundred men stopped work in Culebra Cut, but order prevailed amid a state of general alarm.

Meanwhile strenuous efforts to reorganize were being made in Paris. President Slaven of the American Contracting and Dredging Company was having daily conferences with De Lesseps. Denormandie cabled to the Isthmus that new contracts to assure continuance would be signed.

France assumed a state of "political animation." Meetings of security holders were called throughout the country. At one 5,000 strong, held in a skating rink in Paris, the president of the committee addressed the crowd:

"Shall we leave this glorious work to be completed by foreign powers?"

"*Non, non, non!*" they thundered.

"Shall we agree to forego any return on our investments until the canal is completed?"

"*Oui, oui!*" they replied emphatically.

[25] *Panama Star and Herald*, Jan. 8, 1889.

"Shall we pledge ourselves, each according to his means, to aid this great enterprise by purchasing new shares of Panama stock?"[26]

Again they thundered approval and adopted a resolution covering all points.

In spite of the strongest efforts of De Lesseps and the temporary managers, the movement to organize a new company was frustrated. A last shareholders' meeting was held late in January 1889, when it was decided to request a judicial receiver, and on February 4 the Old Panama Canal Company was dissolved and Joseph Brunet was appointed as liquidator.[27]

The great French effort had expended its force. The savings of French peasants were gone. The company and its officials became the object of attack by both the opposition and the Government. Weakened by age, adversity, and criticisms, the veteran leader of the enterprise had been struck down.

When De Lesseps' directing hand relaxed its hold, there was no one big enough to rally the disillusioned investors and to mobilize another major effort to complete the waterway.

THE LIQUIDATION

The liquidation was painful. In February the last issue of the *Bulletin du Canal Interocéanique* appeared. Brunet made determined efforts to keep work going, but by May 15, 1889, all activity on the Isthmus was suspended after a series of gradual discharges.

Shops were closed, and machinery was slushed with preservative. Dredges were left where they had been working, whether in the low sea-level reaches or in pools near the summit. Excavators, locomotives, and all kinds of rolling equipment were placed on sidings, exposed to rain, sun, and the jungle. Villages along the line lost their population as the unemployed drifted away. The new Colón Hospital became an almshouse

[26] *Panama Star and Herald*, Jan. 12, 1889.
[27] I.C.C., *op. cit.*, II, 21 (U.S.). Paul Bressolles, *Liquidation de la Compagnie de Panama*, p. 20.

operated by Catholic Sisters. Ancon Hospital continued to function, but with the jungle gradually obscuring its statues and crowding out the flowers from its gardens. The areas along the line that had been the scene of so much activity reverted to the jungle, and each year that passed made it more difficult to determine if there had been any effort at all.

Brunet immediately organized a commission to conduct a searching investigation on the ground, by questioning engineers and examining records. Arriving on the Isthmus in the pleasant month of December, the Commission was soon engrossed in activities which did not lack social aspects. At a banquet given by the Director General, the President of the Commission, Aquiles Bergès, was frankly critical. He said that "many questions which should have been previously studied were not examined sufficiently." He considered the fixing of a definite completion eight years previously most unfortunate. He attributed that act of De Lesseps to "complete ignorance" of the conditions on the Isthmus, and his "desire to animate the labors of all."[28]

In the midst of the investigation another casualty occurred to the unfortunate organization. Brunet was taken ill and had to call Achille Monchicourt as coreceiver to assist. Because of failing health he resigned, and he died soon afterward.

The Commission reported on May 5, 1890, that the lock canal could be completed in eight years, that the plant on the Isthmus was in satisfactory condition and sufficient to complete the work, and that the cost to complete would be 580,000,000 francs. It recommended the most careful investigation before starting work and submitted a lock plan.

The liquidation dragged along during the period from 1891 to 1894, the only important work accomplished in Panamá being the collection of hydraulic data on the Chagres. The process was accompanied by great tragedies in the lives of the leaders. The Panama affair precipitated a political crisis in France. The Government, in response to popular pressure, decided to prose-

28 *Panama Star and Herald*, Jan. 6, 1890.

cute those held as responsible, among them officials and directors of the company. Some fled the country. Baron de Reinach committed suicide. Ferdinand de Lesseps and his son,
along with Eiffel, were indicted for alleged corruption.
Charles de Lesseps was arrested to await trial, but Ferdinand
escaped that fate. At the trial, Charles fought valiantly to save
the company and to maintain the integrity of his name. He told
the story of how M. Baïhaut had extorted 375,000 francs from
the company. The President of the Court replied: "You could
have called the police." To this Charles de Lesseps asked: "But
what happens if the gendarme himself is the person holding you
up to ransom?"[29]

Ferdinand, sitting at home, surrounded by his family, was in
a state of mind "from which there is no recovery" and was not
molested. He had only momentary glimpses of passing events.[30]

The struggle was in vain. Both were sentenced to five years,
but the sentences were not executed. Charles lived on until 1923,
but Ferdinand lived only a short time; he died on December 7,
1894, at the age of eighty-nine.

THE NEW PANAMA CANAL COMPANY

The original Wyse Concession was to expire in 1893, and
there was danger of the French losing their franchise. Impressed
by the favorable report of the liquidators' investigation, Monchicourt called upon L. N. B. Wyse to serve Panamá. Again he
was sent to Bogotá, where on December 10, 1890, he obtained
a two-year extension to the concession.[31]

The strenuous work of liquidation wore out Monchicourt,
who died March 14, 1894. He was succeeded by Jean Pierre
Gautron, and the New Panama Canal Company was organized
October 21, 1894, under the name of "Compagnie Nouvelle du
Canal de Panama." One of the conditions imposed by the Old

[29] Siegfried, *Suez and Panama*, p. 279. D. W. Brogan, *France under the Republic*, pp. 268–85, contains description of French political conditions at the time.
[30] H. J. Schonfield, *Ferdinand de Lesseps*, pp. 209–30.
[31] I.C.C., *Report, 1899–1901*, II, 26, 247–50 (U.S.).

Company was the appointment of a Comité Technique to formulate a definite plan for a canal.

The frugality of the French in these years brought about an innovation by the Panama Railroad. With prices of food too high in Panamá, the company in 1894 formed a co-operative grocery store for railroad officials only. The experiment was successful, and two years later its privilege was extended to all employees of the railroad, steamer lines, visiting warships, diplomats, and Canal Company officials. This was the beginning of the tremendous Commissary Division of the Panama Railroad of today.[32]

Relatively, the New Panama Canal Company was a small organization with a capital stock of 650,000 shares of 100 francs each, of which 50,000 paid-up shares were assigned to Colombia. This left a capital of only 60,000,000 francs ($12,000,-000), a sum too small to launch any large-scale work.

When organized, the New Company wanted to retain the French character of the canal and "had no intention or wish to sell their rights on the Isthmus."[33] They wished to establish the value of the Panama Canal as an investment and hoped to reimburse the old investors for their losses. They aimed to realize the dreams of De Lesseps.

On December 9, 1894, the first expedition of employees for the New Company sailed from France; they consisted of a new Director General, Vautard, and twenty employees. Work was resumed in Culebra Cut, as this was excavation that would contribute toward any type of canal which might be adopted. The force grew from about 700 men to a maximum of over 4,000 in 1897.

The New Company quickly appointed an international investigating commission, the Comité Technique, composed of men of the highest professional attainment. One of its members was General Henry L. Abbot, the great student of the Chagres.

[32] *Canal Record*, Aug. 5, 1908, I, 387 (U.S.).
[33] Abbot, *Problems of the Panama Canal*, p. 8.

The Comité Technique arrived on the Isthmus in February 1896. Assisted by an able staff, it made studies to determine the best possible plan. Confident that Nicaragua could not compete with Panamá, they ignored the agitation for Nicaragua then being carried on so vigorously in the United States. Work on the Isthmus was limited to that which would contribute to the final plan and to the collection of data. In contrast to the previous days, "there was no blowing of trumpets,"[34] but instead a meticulous search for facts.

Near the close of the century there occurred the Spanish-American War—which Bemis has called the great aberration in United States history—the Asiatic incursion by the United States, and the spectacular cruise of the "Oregon" around the Horn.

The canal idea was thus dramatized, and the United States demanded complete control of the Isthmian Canal. The logical French realized that these events made their position hopeless. They could not compete with the United States.

The Comité Technique completed its plans on November 16, 1898, exactly three years before the Isthmian Canal Commission was destined to recommend a Nicaragua Canal. The report was the result of three years of study and an extensive examination on the Isthmus. It is interesting because of the evident simplifications which greater knowledge produced.

The canal route remained essentially the same. There were to be two levels, one an artificial Lake Bohío about 61.5 feet above sea level, to be created by a dam at Bohío and reached from the Atlantic level by a double-flight lock. In addition there was to be a summit level 97.5 feet high, also reached by a double flight of locks from Lake Bohío at Obispo. The descent into the Pacific was to be by three locks—a single-stage lock at Paraiso, a double-flight lock at Pedro Miguel, and a single-chamber lock at Miraflores. The canal was to have a bottom width of 98 feet and a depth of 29.5 feet. In dimensions the locks were to be

[34] Abbot, op. cit., p. 6.

738 feet long, 82 feet wide, and about 32 feet deep in the clear. Cost was estimated at $101,850,000. The summit level was to be supplied by a feeder from a lake to be created at Alhajuela (now Madden Lake). A second plan, with Lake Bohío as the summit level and fed directly by the Chagres, was submitted as an alternate.[35]

These plans were designed to meet the problems of controlling the Chagres and the excavation of Culebra Cut. They were the result of a gradual evolution through a series of lock plans.

What would have happened had the Spanish War not attracted the attention of the people of the United States to the Canal idea one can only conjecture. General Abbot, who was familiar with the French documents and was a profound student, stated it as his belief that the Canal would have been completed by the French as just outlined.[36] In that case, there would have been a smaller and perhaps an earlier canal operated along the style of Suez, instead of the great Canal organization we have today.

The company, knowing that its only chance of assuring any return on its investment was to hold on until the United States should take control of the Isthmus, sent a copy of the Comité Technique report to President McKinley, which he received December 2, 1898. During its last years the company limited its excavation to that necessary for holding its concession.

THE FRENCH EFFORT IN PERSPECTIVE

With no other information than that contained in popular books on the Panama Canal, it is easy to minimize the value and extent of French contributions. Many have ignored them altogether, not realizing that the bitter lessons learned by the French supplied the foundation of success by the United States. Nor is it generally known that it was the French effort which determined the location of the first waterway across the Isthmus. The French as the explorers and investigators of the canal route

[35] I.C.C., op. cit., I, 85–86 (U.S.).   [36] Abbot, op. cit., p. 8.

deserve a place at least with other pioneers and builders of the Panama Canal.

The Old Panama Canal Company, under the powerful influence of the great promoter, had launched the plan for a sea-level canal without careful investigation and preparation. When the error was realized, it was too late. Precious time had passed, funds had been expended, and unfortunately the company failed to understand the full magnitude of its task until too late to readjust its plans.

Many reasons have been advanced for the failure of the French—corruption, incapacity, malaria, and yellow fever. There was corruption in certain high places in France, but nothing involving the personal integrity of Ferdinand de Lesseps or his son. There were cases of incapacity, but the French had men of sufficient ability and experience to accomplish the task. There was suffering from malaria and yellow fever, but disease was not the primary cause of failure. In fact disease was almost ignored by the engineers. Yellow fever was never so serious as malaria, a fact well shown by the researches of Dr. Gorgas.

The real reasons for the collapse of the French were their failure to accept the only feasible plan for constructing the Panama Canal, submitted by Godin de Lépinay at the Paris Congress in 1879, and the tragic decision to build a sea-level canal at Panamá without sufficient knowledge of the vastness of the sea-level project. When at last the French Company was forced to change the plan of the canal to a more feasible lock canal, it was too late to avoid a crash. The money of the company had run out, and there was no source to which it could appeal for more funds once it became the object of political attack in France.

At the time when failure became imminent in September 1888, the engineering problems had been largely solved. There were over 14,000 men on the pay roll, and excavation was proceeding at thé rate of about 1,000,000 cubic meters a month,

From *Scientific Monthly*, January 1942. Courtesy of Dr. Gorgas' daughter, Mrs. W. D. Wrightson

GENERAL WILLIAM CRAWFORD GORGAS, 1854–1920
Chief Sanitary Officer, Panama Canal Zone, 1904–1914

with a remaining estimated excavation of only 23,700,000 cubic meters to complete the canal. This would have enabled a completion date in 1891. It should be stated, however, that the canal as planned in 1888 was so small that, if it had been completed, it would have been outmoded even before its completion date.

The new company benefited by the experiences of the old and accomplished its task in a most thorough and scientific manner. It made elaborate studies of canal plans and of Isthmian topography, geology, and hydrology that later proved to be of greatest value to United States engineers. The Isthmian Canal Commission regarded the information as "much more complete than is usual before the inauguraton of an engineering enterprise in a new country."[37] Colonel Goethals later often stated that when he wanted accurate information he went to the French plans.[38]

The total excavation by the two French companies amounted to 78,146,960 cubic yards, of which 11,403,409 was by the new company—a greater volume than the excavation at Suez. Of this total, 18,646,000 cubic yards were taken from Culebra, where the Cut was lowered 333.5 feet to a high point 193 feet above sea level near Gold Hill.[39] The peaks and ridges were removed.

The French left a legacy of tropical buildings and machinery used for many years by the United States. They gained control of the Panama Railroad and developed it as an adjunct to the canal. They developed a splendid hospital service but did not discover the part played by the mosquito in disease and hence suffered by that ignorance. They made fundamental errors in financing and planning. Their equipment was light as compared with later machines, but it is doubtful if North Americans could have done better during the same years. The old Canal Company could have completed its canal had not a combination of circumstances in France destroyed the company and its leaders.

[37] I.C.C., op. cit., I, 86–87 (U.S.).
[38] Dr. J. E. Lefevre, Conversation with the author, Sept. 21, 1941.
[39] Goethals, The Panama Canal, I, 336–37.

It was Ferdinand de Lesseps who paid most heavily for the collapse. Instead of coming to his assistance, the Government "abandoned him in a cowardly way, and then shamefully trampled on him."[40] Four years after his death the French nation erected at Port Said a massive statue of the Canal Builder, with his hand pointing toward the East. The United States later named one of its forts guarding the Atlantic entrance in his honor.

It is impossible to read the detailed history of the French effort without feeling the power of De Lesseps' influence, without understanding how he was acclaimed "The Great Frenchman," without knowing that as "The Great Frenchman" he will remain.

[40] Siegfried, *Suez and Panama*, p. 283.

Chapter VII

THE UNITED STATES TAKES OVER THE TASK

We have not the slightest intention of establishing an independent colony in the middle of the State of Panama, or of exercising any greater governmental functions than are necessary to enable us conveniently and safely to construct, maintain and operate the canal, under the rights given us by the treaty.—Theodore Roosevelt.[1]

THE FIRST COMMISSION ORGANIZES FOR WORK
UNDER ADMIRAL WALKER

For almost fifteen years the Isthmian jungle grew thicker over rusting French machinery, but the hopes of the enthusiasts for resumption of the Panama Canal never faltered. The dramatic cruise of the "Oregon" around the Horn in 1898 centered public attention on the Isthmian Canal idea, and negotiations for a canal treaty were started between Colombia and the United States. After prolonged diplomatic discussion, the Hay-Herrán Treaty was signed with general acclaim and ratified by the United States Senate. In Colombia it was rejected, to the great dismay of all friends of Colombia and the Canal.

Then, suddenly, came the Panamá Revolution of November 3, 1903, and the declaration of independence from Colombia by that young republic, the diplomatic intervention of Theodore Roosevelt, and the negotiation of another treaty by Philippe Bunau-Varilla with an audacity and adroitness that startled Panamá and aroused enthusiastic interest in the United States.[2]

Roosevelt's impulsive diplomatic intervention, done under the impetus of the westward expansion of the United States into the Pacific, was an event of far-reaching consequences. It had wide repercussions in Latin America and did not escape notice

[1] Roosevelt to Secretary of War, Oct. 18, 1904. (The Panama Canal Record Bureau, File 28-I-62; hereafter designated as P.C. Rec. Bur.) (MS).

[2] M. P. DuVal, *Cadiz to Cathay* (chapters x to xii, pp. 255–316) contains a detailed account of these complicated negotiations.

by Japan. But by it Roosevelt undertook to build the Panama
Canal and became the leader for this great enterprise in the
United States. Thus, upon his shoulders fell the mantle of De
Lesseps.

After the ratification of the Hay–Bunau-Varilla Treaty, Roosevelt looked over the list of available men to build the canal
and appointed the seven-man Isthmian Canal Commission as required by the Spooner Act of 1902.[3] He selected a group of
high-grade men—men of strong personalities. Admiral John G.
Walker, who had headed the earlier exploring commission, was
chairman. General George W. Davis, a retired Army officer,
was designated as Governor of the Canal Zone. The engineer
members were William B. Parsons, Benjamin M. Harrod, William H. Burr, and Carl E. Grunsky. Frank J. Hecker was a business man. It was an Army, Navy, and civilian commission, with
the civilians in control of engineering. Unfortunately, the dominant members were not experienced in construction or business.
They could not be expected to handle the pressing problems
of employment, planning, and equipment for so large an effort.

The Commission in a body called on the President at the
White House on March 8, 1904. He told them that they had been
selected from the "best fitted" but warned that he expected resignations from anyone who should find the work "too exhausting
and engrossing." He expected them to be equally exacting with
regard to the selection of their own subordinates and not to pay
the slightest attention to political influence in making their appointments.

He singled out "sanitation and hygiene" for special empha-
sis and urged the use of the best medical and sanitation experts.
He wanted a rigorous supervision of expenditures but desired
the employment of the best talent for every need. Finally, he
warned, "What this nation will insist upon is that the results be
achieved."[4]

[3] DuVal, op. cit., Appendix G, pp. 503–7.

[4] Roosevelt, "Instructions to Isthmian Canal Commission, March 8, 1904,"
I.C.C., Proceedings, first meeting, March 22, 1904, pp. 3–4 (U.S.).

The first meeting of the Commission was held in Washington on March 22, 1904. This was followed by daily meetings for a while. The members handled the many details that always fill the organizing days of any new enterprise.

They made a most thorough search among engineers for a chief engineer. A trip to Panamá was arranged, and, after considering the appointment while on the voyage, they decided to offer the position to one of the leading railroad engineers in the United States, John F. Wallace. Thus it was possible for Commissioner Parsons, while still at sea, to write Mr. Wallace on April 3—the first intimation that he was being considered for appointment as chief engineer of the Isthmian Canal Commission.

Accompanied by Colonel William C. Gorgas, the distinguished Army doctor of Cuban fame who had been selected as chief sanitary officer for the Canal Zone, the Commission arrived at Colón on April 5, 1904. They were welcomed by a committee headed by Tracy Robinson, who had welcomed De Lesseps before them.

These men, however, were not the first group from the United States to reach the Isthmus. Already there were Major William M. Black, Lieutenant Mark Brooke, and Civil Engineer A. C. Harper, who with their secretary, Harry D. Reed, had arrived on April 16, 1903, and also Dr. Claude C. Pierce as the first sanitary representative, who arrived December 31, 1903,[5] and had been studying French methods and Isthmian conditions for months.

The Commission set up headquarters at Colón in a building erected for De Lesseps. Major Black and Lieutenant Brooke showed them points along the line. At Culebra the Commission found about 500 employees of the New Canal Company excavating with a few old French steam excavators, loading cars and hauling spoil to near-by dumps. Fresh from the United States, the Commission could see at a glance how the tremendous

[5] Haskins, *Canal Zone Pilot*, pp. 282–83.

advances in engineering efficiency within a few years had rendered the French equipment woefully outmoded.

Although the Spooner Act contemplated a lock canal, they were encouraged to investigate further the practicability of the sea-level canal, as well as to determine the summit level and lock data for a lock canal. After a visit of two weeks they returned to the United States to organize engineering parties, while Dr. Gorgas and his associates made plans for sanitation. It would not be long before the dirt would fly.

ACQUISITION DAY, MAY 4, 1904

In Paris, final arrangements for the purchase of the New Panama Canal Company's rights by the United States had been completed. On the Isthmus, Major Black, not realizing the advanced state of the purchase negotiations, obtained leave of absence and returned to the United States with the Commission. He was naturally ambitious to become chief engineer and to build the Panama Canal.

Apparently without the knowledge of Major Black, Secretary of War Taft, anticipating an early exchange of the properties, authorized Lieutenant Brooke late in April to act in conformity with the instructions he would receive from the United States representative in Paris. On May 3 the instructions came. They directed him to receive all the Canal properties on the Isthmus from the New Panama Canal Company, except the Panama Railroad, and he prepared to take over the following day.

Early the next morning Lieutenant Brooke and Director General Renaudin; W. W. Russell, United States Chargé d'Affaires; Mr. J. W. Lee, Secretary of the United States Legation; Consul-General H. A. Gudger; and Dr. Claude C. Pierce, of the United States Public Health and Marine Hospital Service, were all assembled at the old Grand Hotel, which housed the French offices. Brooke read a declaration he had drafted, signed a $40,000,000 receipt to Renaudin for the French Canal holdings on the Isthmus at 7:30 A.M.,[6] and hoisted "Old Glory" over the building—an event that caused May 4, 1904, to become known as Acquisition Day.

This young second lieutenant, just two years out of West Point, cabled his action to the Commission then sitting at Washington and took charge. To the old employees he sent a circular announcing that he had taken possession for the United States and requesting them to continue in their positions.

The new organization comprised 746 employees at a monthly pay roll of $15,000 gold; they were organized into a Director General's Office, Disbursing Office, Sanitary Service, Supply and Material Department, Land and Building Department, and Engineering Department, all reporting to the Director General. Equipment included 2,148 French buildings, numerous files and records, and a tremendous quantity of machinery and rolling stock. The buildings included the magnificent Ancon Hospital, the Administration Building in Panamá City, the Taboga Sanatorium, the Dingler residence (Casa Dingler) on La Boca Road, and the residence of the Director General, used later for many years as the home of the United States Legation in Panamá.

GOVERNOR DAVIS FORMS THE CANAL ZONE GOVERNMENT

In Washington organization matters continued. At the eighth meeting of the Commission on May 6, John F. Wallace was definitely offered the position of chief engineer at a salary of $25,000. He not only accepted the position, effective June 1, 1904, but agreed to maintain a "residence on the Isthmus."[7] Captain George R. Shanton, who had served with Roosevelt as a Rough Rider during the Spanish-American War, was appointed chief of police. He proceeded to recruit a force, largely from ex-service men, and dressed them in the khaki uniform of the Rough Riders—a uniform worn by the Canal Zone Police until 1941.

[6] Governor Davis' Statement, April 2, 1906 (Hearings No. 18, III, 2423-24, 2492-93) (U.S.).

[7] I.C.C., *Proceedings*, eighth meeting, May 5, 1904, p. 40 (U.S.).

Under what department of the United States Government should the Commission be placed? Roosevelt was in favor of placing it directly under the War Department. Admiral Walker and General Davis preferred it to remain as an independent agency under the President. Following the advice of the Commission's counsel, Charles E. Magoon, and based on the precedent of the Philippines, President Roosevelt in an Executive Order of May 9, 1904, placed the Commission under the supervision of the Secretary of War and defined its jurisdiction and functions. He did this because the War Department was the Government agency which had charge of civil works on rivers and harbors.

This order was a powerful document. Not only was it the basis for forming the civil government of the Canal Zone, but it authorized the Commission to legislate for "military, civil, and judicial affairs"[8] until the close of the Fifty-eighth Congress. It vested the Commission with powers necessary to construct the canal, directed that members of the Commission be appointed directors of the Panama Railroad, outlined a Bill of Rights, emphasized sanitation as a matter of prime importance in preparatory work, and apponted Major General George W. Davis as the first Governor of the Isthmian Canal Zone. On the Isthmus the immediate reaction was that it meant "almost autocratic powers"[9] for the Commission.

What were the qualifications of Governor Davis? He had had a distinguished record in the Army, had landed the first regiment in Cuba during the Spanish War, and had organized the military government of the Cuban Province of Pinar del Rio. He had been Military Governor of Puerto Rico and had organized its civil government. He had been civil and military governor in the Philippines. There was no hesitation in selecting a man of his positive attainments or investing him with the authority of

[8] Roosevelt, "Letter to Taft, May 9, 1904." *Executive Orders Relating to the Isthmian Canal Commission, March 1904 to June 12, 1911*, pp. 4–11 (U.S.).

[9] *Engineering Record*, May 14, 1904, XLIX, 623.

managing representative for the Commission until the arrival of a chief engineer.

On the day after the Executive Order was issued, Governor Davis, with the first permanent party consisting of Major Black, Ernest Lagarde, Jr., Paymaster E. C. Tobey, Dr. R. L. Sutton, Captain Shanton, and M. E. Mitchell, sailed for the Isthmus. Arriving at Colón on May 17, 1904, they were greeted by a boarding committee, with Tracy Robinson among the welcomers. M. G. de Paredes, reflecting the rising hopes and joy of the Isthmians, addressed General Davis and declared that the time had come to transfer the struggle "from the forum to the field; from the Capitol to the jungle," for a contest with the forces of Nature. Confidently he declared the "clang of the dredge, the boom of the blast, the clatter of the work trains, multitudinous steam whistles, and the glare of thousands of electric lights at night shall be as bugle and drum"[10] for the determined attack. The General replied that he had always been a man of action and that he hoped to measure up to expectations—as was to be found out very quickly.

General Davis did not go to Panamá City until two days later. As Governor, he issued a proclamation of occupation for the Canal Zone and appointed civil officers in the Canal Zone Government. As managing representative of the Commission, he outlined the work of the Canal departments: Engineering under Major Black; Secretariat under the First Executive Secretary, Harry D. Reed; Accounts and Material under Paymaster E. C. Tobey; and Buildings and Grounds under an old French employee, C. F. Bertoncini. Operations were to continue under the same general system already in effect, but with United States methods of accountability.

The one permanent activity of the United States that General Davis found on the Isthmus was the Quarantine Service. It dated back to 1893, when officers of the Public Health and Marine Hospital Service were detailed to serve in consular of-

[10] *Panama Star and Herald*, May 20, 1904.

fices in Panamá and Colón to inspect vessels bound for the United States and sign bills of health. When it was observed that Panamá authorities did not enforce quarantine regulations on vessels arriving from infected ports in South America, arrangements were made for these United States doctors to take over the quarantine duties at both terminal cities. Thus the oldest of the construction organizations was placed under the Isthmian Canal Commission.[11]

Rather tardily, Governor Davis made a formal call on President Manuel Amador of Panamá and announced that the United States had taken possession of the Canal Zone and was continuing the great work which had been under way for so long.

Panamá did not like this precipitate and direct action. It loved formality and wanted a celebration. The result was that Governor Davis found himself in his first controversy. Very shortly he received orders to participate in any ceremonies desired by Panamá, but not to invalidate any action he had taken.[12]

The Governor had more troubles. There was a controversy about La Boca, the Panamá Government claiming that port as the port of Panamá City. This was an impossible situation. Davis would not tolerate its exclusive jurisdiction under Panamá and refused to admit that La Boca was a part of the harbor of Panamá. On that basis he negotiated an agreement with the infant republic and prevented what otherwise would have become in later years a source of friction between Panamá and the United States.

He had been directed to carry on as the French before him had done. When time came for the first payday he had no local (Colombia) silver. The paymaster came to him in despair, but nothing daunted this doughty Governor. He ordered: "Post up an advertisement asking for bids"[13] for the required amount, as if the local silver were merchandise, payments to be by checks

---

[11] *Sen. Doc. 286*, 59th Cong., 1st sess. (U.S.).

[12] Davis, *First Annual Report of Governor of Canal Zone*, Nov. 1, 1904 (Hearings No. 18, III, 2466) (U.S.).

[13] Davis' Statement, March 30, 1906 (*ibid.*, III, 2273).

on the Assistant United States Treasurer in New York. The money came rolling in.

Panamá bankers, however, did not like this procedure. They did not like public financing and wanted Davis to follow the French in getting a quotation, obtaining the required amount, and then paying by draft in Paris, with the public in ignorance. They protested and criticized. Their feelings were hurt. One banker promised to supply all money required, but said, "we are not going to bid for it in competition with every Chinaman."[14] Even so, they decided to comply with the Governor's wishes.

Because silver was the money of the Isthmus, native employees continued to be paid in silver. North Americans were paid in gold. Thus gold and silver became the bases for indicating race—gold for white employees and silver for colored. In exchange, one gold dollar equaled two silver dollars.

From the day he arrived until he left the Canal Zone, General Davis was a prodigious worker and probably was the largest single influence in determining the form of the Canal Zone Government.

WALLACE BECOMES CHIEF ENGINEER

Admiral Walker's first major task was to form an engineering organization. Early in May 1904, he appointed as assistant engineers: Boyd Ehle, H. F. Dose, A. B. Nichols, A. C. Harper, and Charles A. List, to lead several engineering survey groups on the Isthmus. These men in turn recommended other engineers, but it was to Boyd Ehle, who had served as assistant chief engineer on surveys in Nicaragua, that Walker turned to recruit the main body.

By the end of the month every steamer from the United States brought engineers. Nichols, with two transitmen, arrived at Colón on June 5, 1904, to make preparations. The main body under Boyd Ehle, with diamond drillers, arrived on June 8 as the first organized contingent of engineers after the

14 *Ibid.*, III, 2273–74.

acquisition. As the parties arrived the engineers were assigned to surveys: List and his party to Colón Harbor, Nichols at Gatun to investigate the practicability of that location for a dam site, Dose at Bohío, Harper at Culebra, and Ehle at Obispo.[15]

But engineers did not come in sufficient numbers. Many young engineers, under the influence of rumors and propaganda, hesitated to leave the security of the United States and before risking the trip wrote to engineering magazines for advice on health conditions.

To answer these pointed criticisms, Colonel Gorgas, upon return from his first visit to the Isthmus, came to the aid of the Commission by publishing an article on "Health Conditions on the Isthmus of Panama."[16] He was not particularly an alarmist, but he feared malaria as the disease on which the "sanitary measures" would depend. He thought that anyone who slept under a mosquito net, drank boiled water, and slept away from the native malaria carriers would be fairly safe. Certain engineering magazines that followed the Canal question closely also assisted the Commission by disabusing timid minds of their fears. The editors knew that the Canal would prove to be a "great training school" from which they might expect "many graduates of distinction." They wrote highly of the Chief Engineer as a man under whom it was a "great fortune to serve."[17]

Indeed, Wallace had a record of which to be proud. By efficient service on the railroads he had risen from rodman to chief engineer. He had handled the transportation of the crowds at the Chicago World's Fair. As chief engineer he had rebuilt the Illinois Central and become its general manager. He had been president of the American Society of Civil Engineers.

When he accepted the position as chief engineer of the

[15] G. M. Wells, Letter to author, Nov. 8, 1944.
[16] *Engineering Record*, June 4, 1904, XLIX, 704.
[17] *Ibid.*, p. 697.

Panama Canal, he conferred with Admiral Walker, who warned him that his tenure of office was as stated in the President's letter of March 8, 1904. But Wallace emphasized that he could not be expected to take orders in such a large work from any and every individual member of the Commission and that he could not give good service unless granted an "absolutely free hand."[18] He feared ideas of the Commission as individuals more than anything else and did not want to have seven superiors instead of one. It was with those reservations that he accepted.

Most of Wallace's background of experience had been in developed territory where the temporary dislocation of large construction projects could be absorbed. He had had no experience on the frontiers where the unfamiliar problems of the mountains and forests, labor and supplies, and climate would have given some insight into the difficulties of conducting a great enterprise in the primeval jungle. He felt, however, that he could obtain the experience that later would make him a valuable member of the Commission, should any changes occur. Admiral Walker was an old man and could not last long. Wallace was looking for higher things.

The first month of United States control was one of rapid transition. The urgent needs of the hour were sanitation, water supply for Panamá and Colón, and a sewer system. Many streets of the cities were quagmires of indescribable filth. But these problems were not all. Temperance organizations in the States descended upon the President in a drive to make the Canal Zone dry. "Friends of Labor" in Washington became interested in the welfare of their fellow workers and started agitation. The American Boycott Association pressed Admiral Walker for an eight-hour day in a land where a ten-hour day had been in use for many years. A controversy developed between Bohío and Colón as to which should be the Atlantic terminal.

As fast as carpenters arrived they were placed at work re-

18 I. E. Bennett, *History of the Panama Canal*, p. 188.

pairing old canal buildings and railroad stations. Railroad shops started repairing cars. The private car and locomotive formerly used by De Lesseps were renovated and used on daily inspection trips by officers of the Commission. Ancon was selected as headquarters for the offices of the civil government.

Two old excavators continued the excavation in Culebra Cut near Gold Hill, where the high point was 193 feet. That was the only place where digging was actually going on and where all who wanted work could obtain it. But hard work was not popular. All wanted to be "watchmen, timekeepers, and foremen,"[19] positions which presented no difficulties in filling at first.

Resumption of work on the Canal aroused keen interest. Sunday excursions became popular, and curious employees and Isthmians explored along the line of the Canal.

The needs of the growing population increased. Food became scarce and expensive. Butter, cheese, and milk could not be obtained. No one stepped up to meet the demands for feeding the new canal diggers, and the demands continued to increase.

As the number of North Americans grew, the canal rapidly lost its cosmopolitan French atmosphere. It was becoming "Americanized" with a rapid crescendo. On June 12, .1904, the *Star and Herald* issued its last three-language edition, only one month and eight days after acquisition of the Canal Zone by the United States.

The hectic speed of the new occupants had a stunning influence on the Isthmus. When Chief Engineer Wallace, with Colonel Gorgas and sixteen nurses for the Ancon Hospital, arrived, there was no celebration. It was a quiet arrival; but Wallace must have been quite apprehensive about his health, for he brought along "fine metallic caskets"[20] to the Isthmus for use if he or his wife died.

[19] *Panama Star and Herald,* June 9, 1904.

[20] Stevens to Secretary of War, March 22, 1906 (P.C. Rec. Bur., File D-5-25) (MS).

Wallace called upon Governor Davis, brought up the question of his responsibility for all engineering work, and informed Davis that he understood the Governor would be responsible only until his own arrival. Davis showed him his commission as managing representative and agreed to turn over the engineering construction work but would hold on to the powers granted him which, he said, "practically leaves me in charge of the work, as I hold the purse strings."[21] They smoothed matters temporarily, and the Governor issued a circular relieving Major Black and announcing Wallace's assumption of duties on July 1, 1904. Major Black returned to the United States.

Wallace lost no time in inspecting the Canal, looking over French machinery and meeting engineers. The conditions he found were jungle and chaos from "one end of the Isthmus to the other" with much unrest among employees. The only excavation he saw was a "small amount of work on which four or five hundred men were employed at Culebra, and they were doing all their work there by hand."[22] They had worked for the French only enough to hold the concession and were kept on by the United States. So insignificant was their effort that even the drilling was by hand. Wallace stated it would have required 200 to 300 years to complete at the rate then in progress.

The machinery that was housed was in excellent condition, but that which had been issued to French contractors was still resting where it had been left the day French work stopped. Jungle had grown around dredges in the sea-level reaches and in the pools of Culebra Cut. Many dredges were sunk along the banks where they had been secured fifteen years before. Trees were growing through the fireboxes of locomotives. Jungle had so covered the tracks that United States engineers continued to discover sections of track in it for many months. The scene he saw was eloquent with the power of the jungle!

The inauguration of the work by Wallace was celebrated in

---

[21] Wallace's Statement, Feb. 5, 1906 (Hearings No. 18, I, 557) (U.S.).
[22] Wallace's Statement, March 20, 1906 (ibid., III, 2013).

a really North American way on the first Fourth of July under United States control. Excursions were run from both Panamá and Colón to Empire for picnics, with bands playing. At Empire, in the midst of wind and rain interspersed with sunshine, there were athletic contests—events strange to Isthmians, but significant of the changes wrought by the North American successors of the French.

THE COMMISSION IN ACTION

Wallace gave his first attention to Ancon Hospital. The grounds were still beautiful but sadly neglected. As the brush was cleared from the gardens, statuary was uncovered; but much of the gardening work of the French Sisters was lost in the indiscriminate process. Buildings were renovated and quarters prepared for the staff. The hospital had to be ready for the sick that were always expected with the arrival on the Isthmus of large numbers of unacclimated. Along the line, where doctors were stationed, dispensaries were established and converted into line hospitals.

The Isthmus was practically without roads at that time, except the most primitive trails. The Old Spanish Trail had disappeared long before under heavy tropical vegetation. Even La Boca Road along the ridge to La Folie Dingler was half overgrown with jungle. Houses were without the essential conveniences, and many had to use candles[23] in the absence of electric power in the Canal Zone.

Wallace desired to create comfortable living conditions for employees and started two hotels, one at Corozal and one at Culebra. Unfortunately, he lacked building material so badly that he could not keep his carpenters busy nor use all his forces. He had to go into the open market for material brought in by schooners.

When requisitions were sent to Washington they were considered by the Commission with all formality, regardless of their

[23] Jessie Murdoch, "Ancon Hospital in 1904 and 1905." Society of the Chagres, *Yearbook 1913*, pp. 43–58.

AFTERMATH IN THE JUNGLE, NEAR TAVERNILLA:

French land excavator. abandoned 1888. The man sitting on top of the crane was First Lieutenant James G. Steese, Corps of Engineers, United States Army

AFTERMATH IN THE JUNGLE, NEAR TAVERNILLA:
French bridge conveyor, span 156 feet

urgency or cost, thus introducing great delays in delivery and adding to the difficulties of the Chief Engineer. But he kept on and employed a supervising architect to plan new buildings and repair the old; also a sanitary engineer to make plans for the Panamá water supply, which were ready by mid-August.

In the United States the press kept up an insistent demand to "make the dirt fly." The public wanted immediate action. Unfortunately, under this clamor Mr. Wallace and the Commission weakened in their original stand for thorough preparation before construction. Wallace started experimental excavations in July to determine the unit costs, and these were carried along for many months, with insignificant yardage. The French Comité Technique had experimented at Culebra Cut and had obtained excavation cost estimates there of 52 to 81 cents per cubic yard, depending on material encountered in the Cut. Abbot felt that Wallace wasted much time and energy because he did nothing except confirm available information.[24] However, he did place orders for some steam shovels, locomotives, unloaders, spreaders, and other new railroad and construction equipment.

From the beginning, Wallace had his troubles with government routine business procedure, better known as "red tape," which he described as a "system gone to seed"[25]—the tendency to consider the way of doing things as more important than the results. One time he wanted to advance money to labor agents. He called in Paymaster Tobey, a man whom he had recommended for that position on the Isthmus, and asked for money. The Commission organization had made Tobey, as chief of materials and supplies, independent of the chief engineer, and he had to comply with certain of its regulations. Wallace pleaded for funds, but Tobey had to ask embarrassing questions before issuing. Wallace did not like to be questioned by a young man of thirty-five years; that was intolerable to a man who was accustomed to issue transportation for thousands without question.

---

[24] Abbot, *Problems of the Panama Canal*, pp. 22–24.
[25] Wallace's Statement, Feb. 7, 1906 (Hearings No. 18, I, 669) (U.S.).

On August 3, 1904, Admiral Walker and Commissioners Grunsky, Burr, and Harrod arrived for the second visit of the Commission, accompanied by their general counsel, Judge Charles E. Magoon. That same evening, at Ancon, they held the twenty-first meeting of the Commission and began a series of sessions as the Canal Zone legislature. Governor Davis left the same day to go to the bedside of his invalid wife in the United States, and Admiral Walker took over the duties of Governor in addition to his position as chairman of the Commission.

The energy which marked the beginning of United States work had not produced the rapid results expected by the Isthmians. Gorgas had expected to complete sanitation within fourteen months, but both he and Wallace met many obstacles. The demand on the Isthmus was for greater powers for both the chief engineer and the chief sanitary officer. Results could not be obtained when they had to depend upon actions by a commission sitting 2,000 miles away!

As the number of employees increased, rents and food prices rose until it became increasingly difficult to live within income. Eating places were few, and no effort was made to provide more. Shortly a partial solution was found when an employee died and left a destitute widow. The division engineer suggested that she run a mess, assigned her a French building, and built tables and benches. Soon there was a "widow mess," then other messes were formed to help tide over the feeding crisis until the hotels could be completed.

The messes had their troubles. There was no cold storage for meat on the Isthmus. All meat was bought fresh from horse-riding peddlers on the streets. There was no ice, no fresh milk, and nothing but tinned butter. Local bread was dirty, and fresh vegetables decayed so rapidly that employees had to depend on canned foods.[26]

Water was the greatest problem of life in the early days. In

[26] J. J. Meehan, "The Early Days." Society of the Chagres, *Yearbook 1913*, pp. 137–47.

the dry season it was peddled along the streets, and a daily bath was a privilege only of the wealthy. W. C. Haskins describes how the same water served a succession of uses—first, washing the children's faces, then laundering articles of wear, then scrubbing stone floors, and finally cleaning the sidewalk. In the wet season water fell in copious volume and was no problem.

It was this atmosphere that confronted any new arrival as he alighted from the train at old Culebra Station near a swamp and received orders to report to the Division Engineer's Office on the hill. He would trudge along a "narrow trail, dense jungle, on a path so muddy" that he seemed to be stepping backwards. At the office he was supposed to receive "six chairs, a bed, three tables, washstand and tin pitcher, and a clothes rack." What he actually received was a cot and a box.

Employees had to find quarters of their own. Rooms that in the United States would rent for $5 a month, in Panamá cost $20—a rate too high for $100-a-month clerks.

The greatest of all complaints was about food. The young canal pioneers, with their appetites sharpened by work in the jungle, were not satisfied with the usual light tropical diet of fruit, bread, and coffee that was served with monotonous regularity by the Isthmians. They tired of crackers, sardines, and salmon at the Chino shops. They wanted a variety of real food, and they wanted more of it. They wanted ice. They wanted better quarters. They wanted excitement.

In every way the Isthmus was an undeveloped country, with few women and children and few diversions. Men wanted to read, but reading at night was almost impossible because of the poor oil or candle lights and the myriads of insects attracted through the unscreened windows. There was nothing for the canal builders to do except go to bed, pull the sheets over their heads for protection, and wait for the next day to come. It was under these conditions that "letters from home had a special meaning," and each mail was awaited with much impatience. It was too early to bring families to the Isthmus.

Many could not or would not stand the monotony, the privations, the climate, and the loneliness. Almost every vessel
returning to the United States carried many back—the tired and
the disillusioned. The frontier on the Panama Canal was no
place for the weak or fainthearted!

Meanwhile, on August 3, 1904, at its twenty-first meeting,
the Commission started daily sessions on the Isthmus at Ancon
with a comprehensive program. It enacted the Canal Zone Code;
and Commissioner Grunsky, an engineer, prepared the Health
Department organization. After Governor Davis returned, the
Commission at its forty-third meeting on August 31 revoked
the instructions to him as managing representative of the Commission and placed Wallace in sole charge of all construction[27]
on the Isthmus.

Governor Davis foresaw the difficulties ahead and tried to
secure appointment of one responsible head on the Isthmus, as
in the French organization, in which the director general had
been supreme. He explained that the French organization was
admirably suited for adoption by the United States. The position of Washington as seat of the United States organization was
not similar to Paris as headquarters for the French Company,
for in the United States there was only one stockholder, with
the Commission as trustee. There were "no securities to place,
nor a hostile press to placate with subsidies."[28] But the Commission would not accept the Governor's views.

After twenty-nine sessions, the Commission completed its
program on September 7, 1904, and departed for New York,
leaving Governor Davis as executive officer of the Commission
and as President Roosevelt's personal representative.

The Commission was extremely conservative in its actions.
It reflected the attitude of Admiral Walker, who, by long years
of study, had become familiar with the history of the Canal and
wanted to avoid pitfalls at all costs. He was an able man but

[27] I.C.C. *Proceedings*, 43d meeting, Aug. 31, 1904, p. 179 (U.S.).
[28] *Ibid.*, p. 185.

had many set ideas about small matters, particularly the necessity for economy. For example, Colonel Gorgas would take requisitions to him to sign. They would discuss matters and conversation would center on economy. Then the old Admiral would say: "Gorgas, there is one thing certain; whether we build the canal or not we will leave things so fixed that those fellows up on the hill can't find anything in the shape of graft after us." The Admiral then would place the requisition in his drawer and let it rest. It may have been this philosophy that formed the basis for the official inertia which caused so much trouble and took so much to overcome.

TROUBLES GATHER

When Admiral Walker arrived in the United States, he was optimistic. He announced that everything on the Canal was ready for real work, health excellent, and sanitary measures taken. Others had different views. Mr. Wallace pointed out, as he left the Isthmus for New York a week after the Commission, that it would be eight months before Panamá even had its water supply.

When Wallace arrived in Washington he checked on requisitions and found the most disheartening conditions. A typical case was that of pipes he had ordered in August. The Commission members could not agree as to details of specifications; but when he said he wanted pipe regardless of specifications, the order was placed with a firm not familiar with the expediting of shipments, and the pipes did not arrive until January 1905. The trenches dug on the Isthmus in the meantime had caved in because of rains. When Wallace tried sending cables to check on filling of requisitions, he was told politely not to cable so much. The Commission presumed that since he had had free cables on the Illinois Central he did not know that cables cost money.[29]

The Commission wanted Wallace to hurry back to the Isth-

[29] Wallace's Statement, Feb. 6, 1906 (Hearings No. 18, I, 589) (U.S.).

mus, but he wanted to go on leave. They acquiesced, and he went
to his home in Illinois. In an interview there he said that the
work would be mapped out and that digging the "big ditch"
would be in full progress by April 1 of the next year. He lec-
tured at the Chicago Press Club, where he commended Boyd
Ehle and his young engineers of the survey parties for the high
quality of their work.

But Wallace did not have well-defined plans for constructing
the canal. He was interested in a sea-level canal, and for that
Culebra was the key. Cutting Culebra, he said, was a railroad
proposition similar to "relocating the Panama Railroad and
reducing its grades, making a big, heavy cut along its line, using
that line as one of the instruments to do your work."[30] It made
little difference, he explained, whether a railroad was laid in
the Cut to carry trains or whether water was run in the Cut to float
steamships. His plan was not written. As he stated: "I had a
regular system outlined in my mind. . . . . Of course, my subordinates did not know what that plan was."[31] He wanted a full
year of experience before putting his plan into writing.

On the Isthmus congestion mounted with every passing week.
There were not enough men to unload ships. Even if there had
been, the railroad did not have enough cars to handle the traffic.
Work along the line continued slowly. Acting Chief Engineer
W. J. Karner made weekly reports to Wallace by personal letters during October and November 1904. Usually they were
typewritten, but at times he had to write at his home in long-
hand by lamplight and amid the insects. But Wallace did not
like to read longhand reports. In one of his replies he compli-
mented Karner on his penmanship but added that his life was
"too short to read long-hand."[32] Karner acknowledged the compliment and explained the reason, but fired back: "You did not
have to read them unless you wanted to."[33] While the corre-

[30] Wallace's Statement, March 20, 1906 (Hearings No. 18, III, 1991) (US).
[31] Wallace's Statement, Feb. 6, 1906 (*ibid.*, I, 600–601).
[32] Wallace to Karner, Oct. 16, 1904 (P.C. Rec. Bur., File D-5-25 [1]) (MS).
[33] Karner to Wallace, Nov. 1, 1904 (*ibid.*).

spondence was going on, so was the work. In spite of the rain, the mud, and the slides, on November 11, 1904, the first United States steam shovel was installed in Culebra Cut.

The first break in the Commission came on November 16, 1904, when Commissioner Hecker resigned because the Panamá "climate" was injurious to his health. Hecker was a businessman who had done good work on the Isthmus and demanded direct business methods. He saw the futility of remaining any longer and decided to leave.

Mr. Wallace returned with his wife from the United States just in time to prepare for receiving Secretary of War Taft, who was then arranging for his first visit to the Canal Zone. The Wallaces made their residence in Casa Dingler, formerly the home of the French Director General, and their house became the social center of the Isthmus.

In the meantime relations with Panamá under Governor Davis' energetic hand had not improved. Secretary Taft arrived at Colón on November 27, 1904, accompanied by Admiral Walker and William Nelson Cromwell, the clever general counsel of the Panama Railroad and formerly of the New Panama Canal Company. Arriving amidst the oratory and receptions of another Isthmian welcome, he found a full program for a distinguished visitor waiting.

Taft was entertained at the Wallace home. The visit gave him his first close observation of the Chief Engineer. He was impressed by Wallace's "earnestness and interest in the work, his ability, his facility of expression, his power of planning ahead, and his experience . . . . on the Illinois Central."[34]

Most of Taft's time was taken up with conferences. Wallace wanted to see Taft alone, but Cromwell was at his front door when they got up in the morning and was with the Secretary until late at night. At last, when Wallace happened to get Mr. Taft alone, Taft interrupted to let him know that he had promised Cromwell to have him present. Wallace stated that he did not

[34] Taft's Statement, April 19, 1906 (Hearings No. 18, III, 2557) (U.S.).

get a satisfactory interview at any time, even though the Secretary was living in his own home. Mr. Taft, however, obtained firsthand information of conditions on the Zone; and he gained the gratitude of Panamá by quickly presenting a "happy solution" to their problem through an Executive Order, issued by direction of the President on December 3, 1904, while Taft was still on the Isthmus. When he left he was given a great send-off. He had corrected all the "wrongs suffered by this young republic through the misrepresentation of certain treaty rights."[35]

After Taft left, Wallace sent him copies of many documents on Isthmian matters and on relations between himself and Governor Davis. He also wrote about the Panama Railroad, of which he thought the chief engineer should be in complete control, recommending that all its stock be obtained for the Government by either purchase or condemnation.[36] He was critical about the seven-man Commission, 2,000 miles away, exercising executive functions. He wanted the Commission reduced to three men—the chief engineer and the Governor on the Isthmus, and the chairman in Washington, all working on purchases, shipping, and labor. The engineers, he thought, should be engineering consultants rather than members of the Commission with executive functions.

In the meantime the Commission continued to hold meetings and to debate and vote on the most trivial expenditures, with each member considering himself individually responsible for each item. Today when one examines the records of those early years, it is difficult to see how anything at all was accomplished in such an atmosphere, and one wonders why that condition was permitted to last so long.

It had become apparent to Secretary Taft that the Commission had not measured up for large-scale construction work and was "clumsy and ineffective." Something radical had to be done. The Commission had been blamed, but Mr. Wallace had

[35] *Panama Star and Herald*, Dec. 8, 1904.
[36] Wallace to Taft, Dec. 5, 1904 (P.C. Rec. Bur., File D-5-25 [1]) (MS).

escaped censure. What did the Secretary of War have in mind? Governor Davis wrote the Secretary that he regarded Mr. Wallace as a "very superior man, and he ought to be retained."[37] He also suggested combining the offices of minister to Panamá and Governor into one office. The purpose of this suggestion was to remove the friction that had developed between him and the United States Minister to Panamá.

A most curious episode of this period was an attack by the medical profession on the Commission. Dr. C. A. L. Reed had served as a real-estate arbiter on the Isthmus in December 1904. Upon his return to the United States, Secretary Taft requested him to study the Isthmus and report on hygienic conditions.[38] Dr. Reed went down again, looked around, saw the conditions and the people, and wrote a report that was most extreme.

Colonel Gorgas was rightfully praised, but the Commission was condemned indiscriminately for every conceivable kind of failure. Dr. Reed resented placing the sanitary department under the Governor, the requirement that medical requisitions be reviewed by others, and having interns at Ancon Hospital. He accused the Commissioners of having petty antagonisms toward the medical service and of placing Canal doctors in cheapening competition with doctors of Panamá. For the yellow-fever cases he placed full responsibility upon the Commission, "more especially upon Mr. Grunsky," and for many other items responsibility was likewise placed "more especially upon Mr. Grunsky." The report read like the emanations of a radical agitator rather than a judicial document expected from a president of the American Medical Association.

Secretary Taft sized up the value of its contents accurately. He forwarded the report confidentially to Admiral Walker for a statement, noting its biased tone. The Commission's reply was a judicial and careful analysis of the points and made Dr. Reed's report appear ludicrous, especially since he had published the

[37] Davis to Taft, Jan. 6, 1905 (ibid.).
[38] I.C.C., Proceedings: Circular No. 10, Jan. 10, 1905, p. 473 (U.S.).

article in the *Journal of the American Medical Association* without official authority.[39]

EVENTS FORCE RESIGNATION OF FIRST COMMISSION

Early in 1905 work improved at Culebra. Two French excavators and two United States steam shovels were working, with spoil being sent to near-by dumps. The force had increased from 500 men in July to 1,200 in January. The "battle of the levels" was starting. The relative merits of the sea-level and lock canals were being discussed, but Wallace refused to state his views publicly. He appealed, however, for patience and careful preparation of a plan for an undertaking which had required over four centuries "to conceive in the womb of civilization."[40]

While Wallace was writing to the Secretary of War his letters so critical of the Commission's methods, the Canal employees wrote letters critical of conditions in the Canal Zone. They claimed to have been lured to the Isthmus with glamorous promises, but upon arrival found so many inconveniences that they became "homesick and disgusted," particularly when required to live six in a room. They wanted an occasional pleasant evening.

On January 24, 1905, two members of the Committee on Engineering, Parsons and Burr, arrived on the Isthmus. Because of his office, Governor Davis automatically became a member. The Committee examined the Canal and held daily hearings in the Governor's Office, always attended by Wallace, who supplied reports from field parties. While the Committee was inspecting Cristóbal Harbor on January 27, it encountered a severe norther that had begun on the preceding afternoon. Ships at anchor had to go to sea for three days while great waves rolled into the harbor, breaking over the entire water front in

[39] C. A. L. Reed, "Report to the Secretary of War *Showing How the Commission Makes Efficient Sanitation Impossible*," March 2, 1905. I.C.C. *Sanitary Conditions on the Isthmus*, pp. 38–63 (U.S.). Text of Reed's Report and the Commission's Reply.

[40] *Panama Star and Herald*, March 12, 1905.

deluges of water and coral that blocked the streets. The seas endangered the piers. Vessels which could not get under way and go to sea had to secure themselves far enough from the docks to roll and pitch alongside without danger. The Committee had no choice except to recommend a breakwater from Toro Point to the Colón light, as stated in its Report of February 14 to Admiral Walker.[41]

Yellow fever first became a subject of discussion among employees about November 1, 1904; but it was not until the following February that the Panamá press became alarmed at conditions on the Canal and in turn did its best to alarm employees. "Discontent reigns supreme"[42] from one end of the Canal to the other, was the lead in an editorial which announced that President Roosevelt was displeased and that changes were probable. A few cases of yellow fever were given wide publicity in the United States. Exaggerated reports served to keep men from coming to the Isthmus for work.

Mr. and Mrs. Wallace drove about the streets of Panamá to quiet the rumors, but to no avail. The press continued its campaign: "Resignation; transportation; humiliation and consternation. But what can we do? Such is life in the tropics."[43]

Governor Davis cabled Secretary Taft that press reports were "cruelly exaggerated." He deplored the fact that the Commission had not spent most of its time on the Isthmus so the members could realize that the canal was being built on the Isthmus. "Every day, every week and every month the conditions here are improving, little by little."[44] He blamed the agitation on the sensational journals. He knew there was no factual basis for the attacks by the press. He also knew that the end of the first Commission was approaching rapidly.

Wallace later reported that housing conditions had shown marked improvement. In his thirty-five years of experience he

[41] I.C.C., *Proceedings*, 80th meeting, Feb. 9, 1905, p. 375 (U.S.).
[42] *Panama Star and Herald*, Feb. 9, 1905.
[43] *Ibid.*, Feb. 14, 1905.
[44] Davis to Taft, Feb. 14, 1905 (P.C. Rec. Bur., File D-5-25 [1]) (MS).

had never seen any construction men "better housed or any better fed." He said that the ones who complained the most were
those who had obtained their ideas of Panamá from the theater
prior to arrival and that "they expected to swing in a hammock
and sip mint juleps and smoke cigarettes and be fanned"[45] all
day. Nor did employees enjoy the "semi-military rule" of Governor Davis. They wanted civilian control.

Without question, there had been great difficulty in getting
competent men from the States. The United States Civil Service
was no help, but rather a hindrance. In one instance twenty-five
track foremen were requested; but when they arrived, Wallace
estimated that not over two could drive a railroad spike. The
only transportation experience of one had been on pack trains.
Gradually the ranks of subforemen were filled with inefficient
men who could not accomplish results, but who were retained
simply because there was no other recourse.

One of Wallace's largest problems was the Panama Railroad.
He knew from the start that the road would never be able to
meet expected demands with its locomotives, cars and equipment,
and leaders. He had a controversy with the old superintendent,
J. R. Shaler, who was relieved by another old employee, H. G.
Prescott. Warehouses were filled. With the arrival of steadily
increasing quantities of freight the railroad proved incapable
of handling the traffic, and severe congestion resulted. Would
the new superintendent prove competent to handle the crisis?
Wallace said it would take time to determine whether he was
"broad enough, and has the ability to grasp the situation and give
results."[46]

There was nothing to do except to secure complete control
of the Panama Railroad. In January 1905 there were still 1,013
shares of stock outstanding in a total of 70,000 shares, the
United States Government having obtained 68,987 shares from

[45] Wallace's Statement, Feb. 6, 1906 (Hearings No. 18, I, 611) (U.S.).

[46] Bristow, *Report of Special Panama Railroad Commissioner to the Secretary
of War, June 24, 1905*, p. 238 (U.S.).

the New Panama Canal Company. Acting on Wallace's suggestion, Secretary Taft directed the Company's counsel, Mr. Cromwell, to buy the stock at par plus 5. Cromwell circularized the
holders in the United States, England, France, Italy, and elsewhere. He urged them to take advantage of the generous offer,
but made an implied threat of legal proceedings if they did not.[47]
The threat had the desired effect. Late in March, Cromwell
reported that he had obtained all the stock, whereupon he received Taft's commendation for the "patriotism and unselfish-
ness"[48] prompting his action in securing the stock and his refusal
to be compensated. With ownership by the United States complete, the Panama Railroad, financially, had become an adjunct
of the Canal.

Then, suddenly, Wallace was notified that he was appointed
general superintendent of the Panama Railroad. What he
wanted was to be general manager, with Prescott continuing as
superintendent because of his long service. Wallace did not
want to report to the vice-president of the railroad in New York.
That, he said, "would be beneath my dignity,"[49] having held
more responsible positions on railroads in the United States.
He protested strongly to Secretary Taft and Admiral Walker,
asserting his desire to give the "most perfect and loyal service."[50]

The old Admiral was generous and frank. The first he knew
about the appointment was Wallace's cable from the Isthmus.
He considered the action irregular and held matters in abey-
ance. The entire affair had been engineered by Cromwell.[51]

The Isthmus began to wear on Wallace. He heard rumors
of employing a $100,000-a-year man, much his junior in age
and achievements, to take charge and build the Canal. This was

[47] Cromwell to Stockholders of Panama Railroad, Jan. 17, 1905; quoted in his
Statement, May 11, 1906 (Hearings No. 18, IV, 3136, 3140–41) (U.S.).

[48] Taft to Cromwell, March 29, 1905; quoted in Cromwell's Statement, May 10,
1906 (ibid., IV, 3128).

[49] Wallace to Taft, March 21, 1905 (P.C. Rec. Bur., File Personnel, Wallace)
(MS).

[50] Wallace to J. G. Walker, March 21, 1905 (ibid.).

[51] Walker to Wallace, March 25, 1905 (ibid.).

no idle rumor, for President Roosevelt wanted Elihu Root to head the canal work. He had even written to Taft, indicating his willingness to employ Mr. Root at a salary of $50,000 or $100,000 a year which, he stated, he would "cheerfully give him to take complete charge and run this whole business."[52]

Anxiously, Wallace wrote to Secretary Taft that there could be no harmony in such an eventuality and that he had given up a fine home and civilization for that "God-forsaken country" to help him and Roosevelt "in carrying out this great work." As to his own personal desires for such a position he stated, "I do not ask it, am not after it, and prefer to be on the firing line."[53] To Admiral Walker he confided that he had worked too hard and that he wanted to go on leave in May or June, as he would have to recuperate before starting a second year.

In the preceding January President Roosevelt had decided that the Commission should be changed. The seven-man board was "inelastic and clumsy."[54] On January 13, 1905, he sent a special message to Congress, recommending more power to the President and a reduction of the Commission to five or preferably three members, but asking Congress not to restrict them to Army or Navy engineers, as he then had an "excellent engineer." Roosevelt discerned the future clearly. He doubted that Congress would act upon his recommendations and planned to secure his aims by changing the personnel on the Commission. In early February of 1905 the first Commission was on its way out of office, for the President wrote to Mr. Taft, "I am afraid Walker will have to go."[55]

As recommended by the President, the House of Representatives passed a bill embodying his plan, but the Senate refused, and Congress adjourned with no action. This failure to act left the Canal Zone with no government, for the authority of the

[52] Roosevelt to Taft, Feb. 4, 1905 (Taft Papers: Taft-Roosevelt, Box II) (MS).

[53] Wallace to Taft, March 15, 1905; quoted in Taft's Statement, April 19, 1906 (Hearings No. 18, III, 2706-7) (U.S.).

[54] *Messages and Papers of the Presidents*, XVI, 6938 (U.S.).

[55] Roosevelt to Taft, Feb. 4, 1905 (Taft Papers: Taft-Roosevelt, Box II) (MS).

Commission as a legislature under the Act of April 28, 1904, terminated when the Congress which enacted the law expired on March 4, 1905.

Thwarted in their plans by the inaction of Congress, Roosevelt and Taft cabled Governor Davis to continue the Canal Zone Government on the same basis as before Congress failed to act. To Mr. Wallace, on March 24, 1905, he cabled his plans for the reorganization, adopting practically all of the Chief Engineer's ideas. Wallace was elated. He pictured an organization with the real power embodied in an Executive Committee, each member being in supreme charge of a department, the chief engineer and the Governor residing in the Canal Zone and the chairman, as purchasing agent, staying in Washington. On the following day he cabled the Secretary: "Plan excellent. Satisfactory. *Gracias.*"[56] This was strange, coming from a man afraid of yellow fever, who already had intimated his intention to resign.

Now it was only a question of time when the reorganization would occur. It had been generally expected that the Commission members would resign. However, they did not, but worked assiduously, ignoring the attacks. Yet their fate was sealed. Secretary Taft and the President had decided, and Mr. Taft ordered Wallace to come to Washington. He wanted him there to assist in the reorganization.

In Washington, the Walker Commission of Construction carried on as if nothing had happened and held its ninetieth and last meeting on March 29, 1905.

It had performed an enormous volume of preparatory work. It had studied sanitation. It had organized a government. It had recruited the nucleus of a construction force. But as an executive body it had not proved equal to the demands of preparing for a great construction enterprise. It could not supply materials with promptness. The members had been the victims of bad advice and of misrepresentation by the press. Their methods

56 I.C.C., *Minutes*, 98th meeting, July 1, 1905, p. 31 (U.S.).

were not "businesslike, expeditious, or systematic." At the request of the Secretary of War, the Commission resigned.

Wallace's reputation had been built up tremendously by the press. John Barrett, the United States Minister to Panamá, joined the chorus of approval with an article which appealed for confidence in Wallace and opposed placing the work under Army engineers. He contended that "few if any Army engineers have ever had such broad experience and training"[57] as Mr. Wallace. The bulk of resentment was solely against the Commission for its "red tape" and its delays.

As Mr. Wallace left the Isthmus on March 30 for Washington the purpose of his visit was understood by all and much was expected from him. He was acclaimed as the "man behind the gun."

[57] *Panama Star and Herald*, Feb. 22, 1906.

CULEBRA CUT NEAR GOLD HILL, DECEMBER 1904
Steam shovel excavating and loading spoil into French dumpcars

CHAPTER VIII

REORGANIZATION, RESIGNATION, AND CHAOS

Mr. Wallace was not an aggressive man, and there are times and conditions when fighting becomes a righteous duty. The situation which had developed at the date of his resignation was such as demanded a one-man control, control by a man who was heedless of his technical reputation; and one only bent upon smashing a way through all obstacles, a kind of politic "roughneck," who did not possess too deep a veneration for the vagaries of constituted authority.—JOHN F. STEVENS, Chief Engineer of the Isthmian Canal Commission, 1905–1907.[1]

ROOSEVELT APPOINTS A SECOND COMMISSION

Wallace had attained a wide reputation as the first chief engineer of the Panama Canal and had passed through the ordeals of the first Commission unscathed. He had the support of such men as Governor Davis, who wrote directly to Secretary Taft in his behalf, and his retention was decided upon. As Wallace was a railroad man, Roosevelt looked to the railroads—the great constructing agencies in the United States—for a chairman of the reorganized Commission. A man with proper qualifications was found in Theodore P. Shonts, President of the Clover Leaf Railroad. He had been engaged in construction and operation of railroads for many years and was considered a hard-hitting businessman. He was endorsed by many leaders in the railroad world, and was selected because he was thought to be on friendly terms with Wallace.[2] The two men had been schoolmates in their early years.

But Mr. Shonts could not be attracted for less than $30,000 a year. That appeared a high salary, and other men with proper abilities were available, but they demanded large pay. Later, Secretary Taft explained, "They did not have the reputation, the skill, and experience, unless you paid them a salary."[3] Shonts,

[1] J. F. Stevens, "The Panama Canal," A.S.C.E., *Transactions*, XCI, 949.
[2] Taft's Statement, April 19, 1906 (Hearings No. 18, III, 2557) (U.S.).
[3] *Ibid.*, April 21, 1906 (III, 2773).

however, was the type to do his utmost on a task when once he had accepted. As he said, "I am going to put the best I've got in me into it—and I think right now I'm better than I ever was before in my life."[4]

When plans for the reorganization were ready, Secretary Taft forwarded the resignations of the first Commission to the President, with recommendations embodying many of Wallace's ideas. He wished the executive work of the succeeding Commission to be divided into departments, with sanitation retained under the Governor. He wished the seat of power to be on the Isthmus with meetings of the Commission there, and an executive committee resident on the Isthmus with power to act for the Commission in its absence.[5]

Roosevelt covered the appointment and duties of the second Commission in an Executive Order of April 1, 1905. Shonts was designated as chairman, Charles E. Magoon as Governor of the Canal Zone, and Wallace as member and chief engineer. Other members were Rear Admiral Mordecai T. Endicott, Brigadier General Peter C. Hains, Colonel Oswald H. Ernst, and Benjamin M. Harrod. The work was divided into three departments: first, Fiscal Affairs, Purchasing, and General Supervision under the chairman in Washington; second, Government and Sanitation under the Governor; and third, Engineering and Construction under the chief engineer.

All of these men were well known in their fields. Magoon had been in intimate association with Secretary Taft and had been former Secretary Root's chief adviser on island government; he was also well versed in Canal organization. It is no wonder that when announcements of these appointments, with a successful businessman as executive head of the Canal, were made in Panamá they were hailed as marking a new beginning.

The second Commission of Construction held its first meeting in Washington on April 3, 1905, accepted resignations of

---

[4] *Panama Star and Herald,* May 7, 1905.
[5] Taft to the President, March 30, 1905 (I.C.C. *Minutes,* 91st meeting, April 3, 1905, pp. 7–10) (U.S.).

EPILOGUE

Three decades have passed. The Panama Canal has assumed the appearance that comes with age. The ranks of the Canal builders have thinned. Only a few are left who can appreciate the great efforts that were required to build the Canal and to evolve the organization under which it operates.

As vessels transit the Canal, the old French Canal north of Gatun is passed almost unnoticed. The weather-stained locks bear the marks of antiquity. Gatun Dam blends with the landscape. Gatun Lake hides most of the work of the railroad pioneers and of the French and North American Canal builders. Culebra Cut, with its green banks, presents a luxuriant beauty that harmonizes with the surrounding jungle.

When vessels pass through the Canal, the gazers do not recognize the vegetation-covered French and North American dump terraces near the banks of Culebra Cut, the upper French levels on Gold Hill overgrown with brush, or the few abandoned hulks of French dredges that remain as dim marks of a past era. They do not see the sites of vanished towns—Culebra, Empire, or Gorgona—where a few foundation pillars, protruding above the growth, and occasional palm trees are the sole remaining evidences of their previous existence. But there is the same eternal panorama of the tropics, with its irregular mountains, its shades of green, and its brilliant flowers.

Culebra Cut, when seen from one of its high banks in the cool of the tropical night, is a sight that can never be forgotten. Red and white bank lights pulsate at each turn in the channel. Green range lights, marking the center line of the reaches of the Cut, guide vessels as they slowly pass. There is profound silence and calm, disturbed only by whistle signals of vessels rounding turns in the Cut, the rustle of leaves in the light breeze,

339

or the euphonious nighttime sounds of insects, birds, and animals—the symphony of the jungle.

The long history of the building of the Panama Canal and its
operation has been marked by a series of crises in war and peace
that at times have endangered its organization or smooth operation. So far these crises have been overcome. But the Canal still
has its detractors and supporters. There are also the patriotic
who visit the Isthmus for a few hours and, without any background at all, return home to advocate irrelevant schemes for
improving the Canal, such as changing to a sea-level canal or
transforming the Panama Railroad to standard gauge. At times
these problems have been critical. Elements productive of other
crises yet remain, and more crises will come.

The Government of the Canal Zone must remain strong. It
must remain flexible to the requirements of both war and peace.
In war, the military control in defense of the Canal should be
paramount. In peace, the Panama Canal as a great enterprise
serving the shipping of the world must predominate on the
Isthmus.

Building the Panama Canal was not the work of any one man,
but of many men, some of whom were pre-eminent. In building
the Panama Railroad there were John L. Stephens, the founder,
and George M. Totten, the chief engineer.

It was Ferdinand de Lesseps, the French genius and builder
of Suez, who had the vision of building the Panama Canal and
started that great undertaking but did not have the means to
realize his aim. It was Adolphe Godin de Lépinay who, in 1879
at the Paris Congress, contributed the fundamental concept of
the high-level canal with a summit-level terminal lake on each
side of the mountains, joined by an open channel cut across the
continental divide.

Henry L. Abbot, consulting engineer of the New Panama
Canal Company, member of its Comité Technique and later of
the International Board of Consulting Engineers of 1905 for
the United States, was the student of the Chagres whose work

was indispensable for securing adoption of the high-level lock-canal plan.

Philippe Bunau-Varilla, while working on the Canal as a young man in the days of the Old Panama Canal Company, saw the destruction of the French effort. He made the vindication of the name of De Lesseps and the resurrection of the Panama Canal the aim of his life. He maneuvered the Panamá Revolution of 1903 to the advantage of the United States and was author of the Hay–Bunau-Varilla Treaty, by which the United States acquired the Canal Zone.

John F. Wallace, as the first chief engineer for the United States, gathered the nucleus of the construction forces, broke the ground, and discovered the hardships and perils of building the Canal.

The first year of United States effort almost met disaster. It was the eminent engineer and railroad builder, John F. Stevens, whose fertile mind rescued the Canal from chaos and defeat. He organized the railroad-transportation system, brought about the great decision to build a high-level lock-type canal with a dam at Gatun, instead of attempting a sea-level canal. He created the fundamental organization under which the Canal was constructed.

George W. Goethals, as the great administrator, had the power and determination to overcome the inertia of routine government procedure and to see the task through to the end, and thereby won fame as the builder of the Panama Canal.

It was William C. Gorgas who, throughout the entire construction period under the United States, as guardian of the Canal builders and the great leader of sanitation, contributed so much to the success of the effort.

Jackson Smith, as organizer of labor, quarters, and subsistence, was largely responsible for assembling the construction forces. William L. Sibert, builder of the Atlantic locks and Gatun Dam, Sydney B. Williamson, builder of the Pacific locks, and L. K. Rourke, organizer of excavation in Culebra Cut, were the chief construction engineers during the United States effort. H. F. Hodges originated many unique electrical innovations in the locks of the Panama Canal. Of all the constructive builders, none contributed more than Sibert and Stevens.

The opening of the Panama Canal to traffic in 1914 symbolized the completion of the greatest engineering work in the history of mankind—a work that brought fame to its builders and continues to be a source of national pride. But the Canal, when opened to traffic, was not complete. The builders knew that the canal project was so vast it could never be completed.

The plan of the Panama Canal had been developed from years of engineering studies. It had not been evolved from marine operating experience. The form for the final canal had not been determined. The great marine operating problems of the Panama Canal had not been clearly recognized. They remained as problems for which only years of marine operations could supply the solution.

THE FUTURE CANAL

The author was stationed on the Isthmus as Captain of the Port of the Pacific Terminal from March 5, 1941, to June 30, 1944. This was the most critical period in the history of the Panama Canal, and it afforded him an exceptional opportunity to observe and study the marine operations of the canal during both peace and war.

His studies conclusively demonstrated that the Panama Canal as completed in 1914 contained a fundamental error in operational design. That error was the location of the Pedro Miguel Locks at the south end of Culebra Cut and the resulting absence of a summit-level anchorage on the Pacific. This arrangement caused the great traffic bottleneck of the Panama Canal to be at Pedro Miguel.

Based upon his studies and repeated operating experience, the author developed and submitted a plan for the fundamental simplification and improvement of the Panama Canal. He pre-

APPENDIX

Appendix A

UNITED STATES ISTHMIAN CANAL COMMISSIONS

ISTHMIAN CANAL COMMISSION FOR EXPLORATION, 1899-1901

REAR ADMIRAL JOHN G. WALKER, U.S.N., Retired, *President.*
COLONEL PETER C. HAINS, U.S.A., Retired.
LIEUTENANT COLONEL OSWALD H. ERNST, U.S.A.
SAMUEL PASCO.
ALFRED NOBLE, C.E.
GEORGE S. MORISON.
WILLIAM H. BURR, C.E.
LEWIS H. HAUPT, C.E.
EMORY R. JOHNSON.

ISTHMIAN CANAL COMMISSIONS FOR CONSTRUCTION, 1904-1914

First Isthmian Canal Commission, Appointed March 8, 1904

REAR ADMIRAL JOHN G. WALKER, U.S.N., Retired, *Chairman.*
MAJOR GENERAL GEORGE W. DAVIS, U.S.A., Retired, *Governor of the Canal Zone.*
WILLIAM BARCLAY PARSONS, C.E.
WILLIAM H. BURR, C.E.
BENJAMIN M. HARROD, C.E.
CARL EWALD GRUNSKY, C.E.
FRANK J. HECKER.

Changes

FRANK J. HECKER resigned November 16, 1904.

Second Isthmian Canal Commission, Appointed April 1, 1905

THEODORE P. SHONTS, *Chairman.*
CHARLES R. MAGOON, *Governor of the Canal Zone.*
JOHN F. WALLACE, *Chief Engineer.*
REAR ADMIRAL MORDECAI T. ENDICOTT, U.S.N., Retired.
BRIG. GENERAL PETER C. HAINS, U.S.A., Retired.
COLONEL OSWALD H. ERNST, C.E., U.S.A.
BENJAMIN M. HARROD, C.E.

Changes

JOHN F. WALLACE resigned June 28, 1905.

JOHN F. STEVENS, appointed Chief Engineer, June 30, 1905; member, June 30, 1906; and Chairman, March 4, 1907, to succeed T. P. Shonts.

OSWALD H. ERNST resigned June 30, 1906.

CHARLES E. MAGOON resigned September 25, 1906, without relief.

JACKSON SMITH, appointed February 14, 1907.

WILLIAM C. GORGAS, appointed February 14, 1907.

THEODORE P. SHONTS resigned March 4, 1907; succeeded by John F. Stevens.

GEORGE W. GOETHALS, appointed member March 4, 1907.

DAVID D. GAILLARD, appointed March 16, 1907, to succeed P. C. Hains.

WILLIAM L. SIBERT, appointed March 16, 1907, to succeed M. T. Endicott.

HARRY H. ROUSSEAU, appointed March 16, 1907, to succeed B. M. Harrod.

Third Isthmian Canal Commission, Appointed April 1, 1907; expired March 31, 1914

LIEUTENANT COLONEL GEORGE W. GOETHALS, C.E., U.S.A., *Chairman and Chief Engineer.*

MAJOR DAVID D. GAILLARD, C.E., U.S.A.

MAJOR WILLIAM L. SIBERT, C.E., U.S.A.

HARRY H. ROUSSEAU, C.E., U.S.N.

LIEUTENANT COLONEL WILLIAM C. GORGAS, M.C., U.S.A.

JACKSON SMITH.

JOSEPH C. S. BLACKBURN.

Changes

JACKSON SMITH resigned September 14, 1908.

LIEUTENANT COLONEL H. F. HODGES, appointed September 15, 1908, to succeed Jackson Smith.

J. C. S. BLACKBURN resigned December 4, 1909.

MAURICE H. THATCHER, appointed April 12, 1910, to succeed J. C. S. Blackburn; resigned August 8, 1913.

RICHARD L. METCALFE, appointed August 9, 1913, to succeed Maurice H. Thatcher.

DAVID D. GAILLARD, died December 5, 1913; no successor appointed.

Appendix B

ABBREVIATIONS USED IN FOOTNOTES

The more common abbreviations used are not listed.

A.S.C.E.	American Society of Civil Engineers.
C.Z.	Canal Zone.
Cong.	Congress.
Doc.	Document.
E.S.P.	Engineers' Society of Pennsylvania.
Ex. or Exec.	Executive.
House	House of Representatives.
I.C.C.	Isthmian Canal Commission.
Jt.	Joint.
Misc.	Miscellaneous.
(MS)	Group designation for manuscripts consulted in Library of Congress, National Archives, and The Panama Canal Archives, the latter designated as (P.C. Rec. Bur.).
N.G.	New Granada (now Colombia).
P.C.	The Panama Canal (official name of government in Canal Zone).
P.C. Rec. Bur. ...	Official Archives of the Panama Canal at Balboa Heights, C.Z.
Res.	Resolution (Congressional).
Sen.	United States Senate.
sess.	Session of Congress.
tr.	Translated.
U.S.	Group designation for United States official and semiofficial documents.

Appendix C

REFERENCES CONSULTED

NONOFFICIAL PUBLICATIONS

ABBOT, HENRY L., BRIGADIER GENERAL, U.S.A. *Problems of the Panama Canal, Including Climatology of the Isthmus, Physics and Hydrology of the River Chagres, Cut at the Continental Divide, and Discussion of Plans for the Waterway, with History from 1880 to Date.* (2d ed.) New York: Macmillan Company, 1907.

Addresses at the De Lesseps Banquet Given at Delmonico's, March 1, 1880. New York: D. Appleton & Company, 1880. (Pamphlet.)

AMERICAN SOCIETY OF CIVIL ENGINEERS. *Transactions,* New York, XCI (Dec. 1927), pp. 946–67.

Aspinwall Daily Courier, The, Feb. 24, 1855, Vol. I, No. 14. Aspinwall (Navy Bay), N.G. (Available in Panama Canal Library, Balboa Heights, C.Z.)

AUTENRIETH, E. L. *Topographical Map of the Isthmus of Panama.* New York: J. H. Colton, 1851. (Available in Panama Canal Library.)

BAKENHUS, REUBEN E., HARRY S. KNAPP, AND EMORY R. JOHNSON. *The Panama Canal . . . . Its History and Construction, in Its Relation to the Navy, International Law and Commerce.* New York: John Wiley & Sons, 1915. (By men who had worked on the Canal project.)

BARRETT, JOHN. *The Panama Canal, What It Is, What It Means . . . .* Washington, D.C.: Pan American Union, 1913.

BEMIS, SAMUEL F. *The American Secretaries of State and Their Diplomacy.* New York: A. A. Knopf, 1928. 10 volumes.

BENNETT, IRA E. *History of the Panama Canal; Its Construction and Builders.* (Builders' edition.) Washington, D.C.: Historical Publishing Co., 1915.

BIDWELL, CHARLES T. *The Isthmus of Panama.* London: Chapman & Hall, 1865.

BIGELOW, JOHN. *The Panama Canal and the Daughters of Danaus.* New York: Baker & Taylor Co., 1908.

BISHOP, FARNHAM. *Panama, Past and Present.* (Revised edition.) New York: Century Company, 1916.

BISHOP, JOSEPH B. *The Panama Gateway.* New York: Scribner's, 1913.

BISHOP, JOSEPH B., AND FARNHAM BISHOP. *Goethals, Genius of the Panama Canal: a Biography.* New York: Harper, 1930.

BLYTHE, SAMUEL G. "Life in Spigotty Land; the Cohorts of King Yardage," *Saturday Evening Post,* March 21, 1908.

BRESSOLLES, PAUL. *Liquidation de la Compagnie de Panama; Commentaire ... de la Loi du 1ᵉʳ juillet 1893.* Paris: A. Rousseau, 1894.

BROGAN, DENNIS W. *France under the Republic; the Development of Modern France (1870–1939).* New York: Harper, 1940.

BULLARD, ARTHUR (ALBERT EDWARDS, pseudonym). *Panama, the Canal, the Country, and the People.* (Revised edition, with additional chapters.) New York: Macmillan Company, *ca.* 1914.

BUNAU-VARILLA, PHILIPPE. *From Panama to Verdun; My Fight for France.* Philadelphia: Dorrance & Co., *ca.* 1940.

————. *The Great Adventure of Panama.* Garden City, N.Y.: Doubleday, Page & Company, 1920.

————. "How to Build the Panama Canal?" (Lecture before the National Geographic Society in Washington, Nov. 29, 1905.)

————. *Panama: The Creation, Destruction, and Resurrection.* New York: McBride, Nast & Company, 1914.

CHAGRES SOCIETY. *See* Society of the Chagres.

CLAYBOURN, JOHN G. *Dredging on the Panama Canal.* Privately printed, *ca.* 1931. (Paper presented at first meeting of Panama Section of American Society of Civil Engineers, Feb. 27, 1931.)

COLLINS, JOHN O. *The Panama Guide.* Panama: Vibert & Dixon, *ca.* 1912.

————. *Same.* Published at Mount Hope, C.Z., by Isthmian Canal Commission Press.

CONGRÈS INTERNATIONAL D'ÉTUDES DU CANAL INTEROCÉANIQUE ... DU 15 AU 20 MAI, 1879. *Compte Rendu du Séances.* Paris: Imprimerie Émile Martinet, 1879.

DAVIS, GEORGE W. Article quoted in *Canal Record,* Vol. I (Dec. 25, 1907), p. 133.

DE LESSEPS, FERDINAND. "Discussion" (on Interoceanic Canals, with his answers to questions by J. Dirks), in American Society of Civil Engineers, *Transactions,* IX (March 1880), 89–94, 96, 97, 98.

————. *Recollections of Forty Years.* Translated by C. B. Pitman. New York: D. Appleton & Company, 1888. 2v. in 1.

DuVal, Miles P., Jr., Captain, U.S.N. *Cadiz to Cathay.* Stanford University, Calif.: Stanford University Press, 1940.

———. The Marine Operating Problems of the Panama Canal and the Solution. (Paper presented before the Panama Section of the American Society of Civil Engineers, May 20, 1943.)

Engineering News . . . . , New York, LX (July–Dec. 1908). (Editorial, without title, exposing sources and falsity of criticisms on Gatun Dam design, Dec. 24, p. 717); "Letters to the Editor: Mr. John F. Stevens on the Gatun Dam Design" (Dec. 31, p. 751).

Engineering Record, Building Record, and Sanitary Engineer. New York: McGraw Publishing Company, Vols. XLIX–LVI (various dates, 1904–1907).

Goethals, George W. "Address at Annual Banquet . . . . Hotel Tivoli, March 6, 1915." Society of the Chagres, *Yearbook 1915,* pp. 159–72.

———. "The Building of the Panama Canal." Illustrated from paintings by W. B. Van Ingen . . . . and from photographs. *Scribner's Magazine,* Vol. LVII (March–June 1915).

———. *The Panama Canal; an Engineering Treatise.* McGraw-Hill Book Company, 1916. 2 volumes.

———. *Same.* International Engineering Congress, San Francisco, *Transactions,* 1915, Vol. I, Pts. 1–2, "The Panama Canal." *Paper No. 1,* "Introduction," general view of construction in the three divisions of the Canal, with map, pp. 1–30. *Paper No. 10,* "The Dry Excavation of the Panama Canal," pp. 335–86.

Gorgas, Mrs. Marie C. (Doughty), and Burton J. Hendrick. *William Crawford Gorgas, His Life and Work.* Garden City, N.Y.: Doubleday, Page & Company, 1924.

Gorgas, William C. "Health Conditions on the Isthmus," *Engineering Record,* Vol. XLIX (May 14, 1904).

———. "Sanitary Conditions as We Found Them in 1904." Speech, Jan. 20, 1912. Society of the Chagres, *Yearbook 1912,* pp. 37–44.

———. Reports as Chief Sanitary Officer of the Panama Canal, 1906. *See* Isthmian Canal Commission (U.S.), "Population and Deaths" and "Report of Department of Health for January 1906."

Haskin, Frederic J. *The Panama Canal.* Garden City, N.Y.: Doubleday, Page & Company, 1913. (Illustrated from photographs by E. Hallen, official photographer to Isthmian Canal Commission.)

Haskins, William C., *editor. Canal Zone Pilot.* Panama: Star and Herald Company, 1908.

HESS, LOUIS T., COLONEL, MEDICAL CORPS, U.S.A. "Ancon Hospital, Ancon," *Surgery, Gynecology and Obstetrics*, XXXI (October 1920), 424–29.

HODGES, HENRY F., LIEUTENANT COLONEL, CORPS OF ENGINEERS, U.S.A. "The Panama Canal," in Engineers' Society of Pennsylvania, *Journal*, I (July 1909), 311–39.

INTEROCEANIC CANAL CONGRESS, PARIS, May 1879. *See* Congrès International d'Études du Canal Interocéanique.

KIRKPATRICK, RALPH Z. *Reference Book on the Panama Canal.* July 20, 1939. (Mimeographed pamphlet, available in Panama Canal Library, Balboa Heights, C.Z.)

LIDGERWOOD MANUFACTURING COMPANY, Elizabeth, N.J. *Rapid Unloaders for Discharging Dirt, Ballast, Rock or Ore.* Illustrated catalogue, *ca.* 1919).

LINDSAY, C. T. *A Short History of the Panama Railroad.* Address before Caribbean Chapter No. 21, National Sojourners, Colón, June 17, 1936. (Mimeographed pamphlet, available in Panama Canal Library, Balboa Heights, C.Z.)

London Standard, The, Dec. 8, 1880.

London Times, The, Sept. 7, 1888.

MCCAIN, WILLIAM D. *The United States and the Republic of Panama.* Durham, N.C.: Duke University Press, 1937.

MACK, GERSTLE. *The Land Divided.* New York: A. A. Knopf, 1944.

NATIONAL ACADEMY OF SCIENCES, Washington, D.C. "Preliminary Report [Feb. 4, 1916] upon the Possibility of Controlling the Land Slides Adjacent to the Panama Canal," by the Committee Appointed [Nov. 18, 1915] at the Request of the President of the United States, *Proceedings*, II (April 15, 1916), 193–207.

NELSON, WOLFRED. *Five Years at Panama; the Trans-Isthmian Canal.* New York: Belford Company, 1889.

NEVINS, ALLAN. *Hamilton Fish. The Inner History of the Grant Administration*, with an Introduction by John Bassett Moore. New York: Dodd, Mead & Company, 1936.

New York Herald, March 3, 1880, p. 6. [Editorial] "De Lesseps' Visit to the United States."

New York Tribune, Aug. 16, 1876, pp. 1, 5: "An Invasion of Prerogative." (Message to Congress, Aug. 14.)

OTIS, FESSENDEN N. *Isthmus of Panama. History of the Panama Railroad and of the Pacific Mail Steamship Company.* New York: Harper, 1867. (Published originally in 1861 under the title "Illustrated

History of the Panama Railroad"; second edition in 1862.) Text and
illustrations on the Panama Railroad and Canal are based on Otis'
article entitled "Tropical Journeyings," published under the pseudonym "Oran," in *Harper's New Monthly Magazine*, XVIII (Jan.
1859), 145–69.

PADELFORD, NORMAN J. *The Panama Canal in Peace and War.* New
York: Macmillan Company, 1942.

Panama American, March 20, 1936, pp. 1, 8. (Available in Library of
Congress.)

PANAMA CANAL, THE. *The Panama Canal, Twenty-fifth Anniversary,
August 15, 1939.* Mt. Hope, C.Z.: The Panama Canal Press, 1939.

Panama Canal Record. See Canal Record (U.S.).

Panama Herald. Published by Green & Middleton, Panamá City, N.G.
(Various dates, 1851–1853.) Available in *Panama Star and Herald*
archives.

PANAMA RAILROAD COMPANY. *Panama Railroad Company, Capital
$1,000,000, with Liberty to Increase to $5,000,000.* New York: Van
Norton & Ammerman, Printers, 1849.

Panama Star. Panamá City, N.G. (Various dates, 1853–1854.) Available in *Panama Star and Herald* archives.

Panama Star and Herald. Panamá City, Republic of Panamá. (Various dates, 1854–1907, and Feb. 18, 1927.) Available in *Star and
Herald* archives.

PEPPERMAN, WALTER L. *Who Built the Panama Canal?* New York:
E. P. Dutton & Company, *ca.* 1915.

PIM, BEDFORD C. T., CAPTAIN, R.N. "Remarks on the Panama Canal,
October 1884." (A private and confidential document submitted to
the Secretary of the United States Navy, Nov. 8, 1884; printed, with
the Secretary's permission, in the *Washington National Republican*,
Jan. 20, 1885, with other papers by Pim, under the combined title
"Nicaragua vs. Panama.")

RICHARDSON, ALBERT D. *Personal History of Ulysses S. Grant.* Hartford, Conn.: American Publishing Company, 1885.

ROBINSON, TRACY. *Panama; a Personal Record of Forty-six Years.
1861–1907.* New York and Panama City: The Star and Herald
Company, 1907.

ROOSEVELT, THEODORE. *Theodore Roosevelt; an Autobiography.* New
York: Macmillan Company, 1914.

San Francisco Evening Bulletin, July 16, 1887. [Editorial] "The New
Panama Canal Loan."

SANDS, WILLIAM F., AND JOSEPH M. LALLEY. *Our Jungle Diplomacy.* Chapel Hill, N.C.: University of North Carolina Press, 1944.

SCHONFIELD, HUGH J. *Ferdinand de Lesseps.* London: Herbert Joseph, Ltd., 1937.

SHELDON, R. C. "A History of Construction, Operation, and Maintenance of the Panama Railroad." 1933. (Thesis presented to Ohio Northern University, Ada. Mimeograph copy available in Panama Canal Library, Balboa Heights, C.Z.)

SHONTS, THEODORE P. *Address by the Chairman of Isthmian Canal Commission, Delivered before the Bankers' Club, Chicago, May 24, 1905.* Pamphlet. Available in Panama Canal Library and in Library of Congress.

————. *Speech by the . . . . Chairman of the Isthmian Canal Commission, before the Commercial Club, Cincinnati, Ohio, on the Evening of Jan. 20, 1906.* Washington, D.C.: Government Printing Office, 1906. Pamphlet. Available in Panama Canal Library and in Library of Congress.

SIBERT, WILLIAM L., AND JOHN F. STEVENS. *The Construction of the Panama Canal.* New York: D. Appleton & Company, 1915.

SIEGFRIED, ANDRÉ. *Suez and Panama.* Translated from the French by H. H. and Doris Hemming. New York: Harcourt, Brace & Company, *ca.* 1940.

SMITH, DARRELL H. "The Panama Canal; Its History, Activities and Organization." Brookings Institution, Washington, D.C. Institute for Government Research. *Service Monographs of the United States Government, No. 44.* Baltimore: The Johns Hopkins Press, 1927.

SOCIETY OF THE CHAGRES. *Yearbook 1911–1917.* From 1911 to 1912 published by Isthmian Canal Commission Press, Quartermaster's Dept., Mount Hope, C.Z.; from 1913 to 1914 published by John O. Collins, Culebra, C.Z.; in 1915, edited by John K. Baxter and F. G. Swanson, Press of W. F. Roberts & Co., Washington, D.C.; from 1916 to 1917, edited by F. G. Swanson, Press of Girard Job Shop, Girard, Kans.

STEVENS, JOHN F. *An Engineer's Recollections.* New York: McGraw-Hill Publishing Company, 1936. (Reprinted from *Engineering News-Record,* between March 21 and Nov. 28, 1935.)

————. "The Panama Canal." Address by the President of the Society at the Annual Convention, Denver, Colo., July 13, 1927. American Society of Civil Engineers, *Transactions,* XCI (Dec. 1927), 946–67.

TOMES, ROBERT. *Panama in 1855: An Account of the Panama Railroad . . . . of the Cities of Panamá and Aspinwall, with Sketches of Life and Character on the Isthmus.* New York: Harper, 1855.

WYSE, LUCIEN N. B. *Le Canal de Panama, l'Isthme américain, explorations ... un plan panoramique du Canal de Panama supposé achevé, un tableau synoptique des divers projéts ...* Paris: Hachette et Cie., 1886. (With appendixes of treaties, contracts, etc.)

OFFICIAL AND SEMIOFFICIAL PUBLICATIONS
UNITED STATES*

Designated in footnotes by (U.S.), following the citation.

BOARD OF CONSULTING ENGINEERS ON PANAMA CANAL. *Report (Jan. 10, 1906) . . . . for the Panama Canal* (prefatory letters of transmittal from the President and Secretary of War), 426 pp., 1906.

BOARD OF ENGINEERS Appointed to Accompany ex–Secretary of War . . . . Taft to the Isthmus. *See* Roosevelt, *Isthmian Canal.*

BRISTOW, JOSEPH L. *Report of Special Panama Railroad Commissioner to the Secretary of War, June 24, 1905.* Washington, D.C.: Office of Administration, Isthmian Canal Affairs, 1905.

BURNSIDE, AMBROSE E., GENERAL, U.S.A., SENATOR. "Joint Resolution (Sen. Res. No. 43) in Relation to the Construction of a Canal Across the Isthmus of Darien by European Powers," *Congressional Record,* Vol. IX, Pt. 2, p. 2312. (46th Cong., 1st sess., June 25, 1879.)

Canal Record. Various dates, 1907–1914. illus. tables, diagrs. (The complete set covers Volumes 1–34, Sept. 4, 1907—April 30, 1941. Issued weekly, 1907–June 1933; monthly, July 1933–1941. Published under the authority and supervision of the Isthmian Canal Commission, 1907–March 1914; by The Panama Canal, April 1914–1941. No more published. After August 16, 1916, title is *Panama Canal Record.* Available in The Panama Canal Library, Balboa Heights, Canal Zone, and in Library of Congress.)

COMMISSION OF FINE ARTS. *Panama Canal . . . . Report . . . . of Fine Arts in Relation to the Artistic Structure of the Panama Canal,* 1913. (Sen. Doc. 146, 63d Cong., 1st sess.)

* As each reference in this group was published by the Government Printing Office and by authority of Congress unless otherwise indicated, the phrase "Washington, D.C., Government Printing Office" is not used here. Likewise, the introductory letters, "U.S.," are omitted here and in footnotes.

CONGRESS

Documents:

Senate

No. 102 (58th Cong., 2d sess.). *Interoceanic Canal Congress, Paris,* 1879. Instructions to . . . . Delegates . . . . of the United States . . . . and Reports of the Proceedings of the Congress (June 21, 1879). Ordered printed, Jan. 19, 1904.

No. 286 (59th Cong., 1st sess.). *Quarantine Conditions in the Isthmian Canal Zone* . . . . Letter from Walter Wyman, Surgeon General of the Marine Hospital Service . . . . , March 22, 1906.

*Hearings:**

House Committee on Appropriations

No. 1 (60th Cong., 1st sess.). *Hearings Concerning Estimates for Construction of Isthmian Canal for Fiscal Year 1908,* conducted at Culebra, C.Z., Nov. 11–12, 1907. Printed 1908.

No. 2 (61st Cong.). *Same,* for Fiscal Year 1911, conducted on the Canal Zone, Nov. 17–18, 1909. Printed 1910.

No. 3 (62d Cong.). *Same,* for Fiscal Year 1913, conducted on the Canal Zone, Nov. 20–21, 1911. Printed 1912.

No. 4 (62d Cong.). *The Panama Canal.* Hearings Concerning Estimates for Construction of (Conducted on Canal Zone, Nov. 18, 1912) and Fortification of (Conducted in Washington, D.C., by the Subcommittee in Charge of the Sundry Civil Appropriation Bill, Jan. 16, 20, 1913) . . . . for Fiscal Year 1914. Printed 1913.

No. 5 (63d Cong., 2d sess.). *The Panama Canal 1915.* Hearings Concerning Estimates for Construction of (Conducted at Ancon . . . . , C.Z., Nov. 18–20, 1913) and Fortification of (Conducted in Washington, D.C., by the Subcommittee . . . . , Feb. 23–25, 1914) for Fiscal Year 1915. Printed 1914.

No. 6. Supplement to Hearings before Subcommittee . . . . in Charge of Sundry Civil Appropriation Bill for 1907

---

* All hearings concerning the Isthmian Canal for the fiscal years 1904 to 1915 were consulted, but only those cited in footnotes are included in this list. Where titles of hearings are too lengthy to appear in footnotes, the serial designations are substituted there.

(April 10 to May 9, 1906), Isthmian Canal (May 25–28, 1906). Printed 1906.

No. 7. Hearings (Jan. 5 to Feb. 11, 1907) before Subcommittee . . . . in Charge of Sundry Civil Appropriation Bill for 1908. Printed 1907.

No. 8. Supplement to Hearings before Subcommittee . . . . in Charge of Sundry Civil Appropriation Bill for 1910 . . . . , Isthmian Canal (Feb. 15–16, 1909). Printed 1909.

No. 9. Hearings (Jan. 13–15, 1906) before Subcommittee . . . . in Charge of Deficiency Appropriations for 1906 and Prior Years on Urgent Deficiency Bill. Printed 1906.

House Committee on Interstate and Foreign Commerce

No. 10. Hearings (June 5, 1906) . . . . on the Isthmian Canal. Printed 1906.

No. 11. Hearings (Jan. 14, 1906) . . . . on Panama Canal. Printed 1908.

No. 12. Hearings (Jan. 6–7, 1909) . . . . on Panama Canal, Hotel Tivoli, Ancon, C.Z. Printed 1909.

No. 13. Hearings (Feb. 11, 1911) . . . . on the Bill H.R. 31436, Operation of Panama Canal, etc. Printed 1911.

No. 14 (62d Cong.). Hearings . . . . on Operation of Panama Canal, etc. . . . . , June 7, 1911. Printed 1911.

No. 15 (62d Cong., 2d sess.). *The Panama Canal.* Hearings . . . . (at Ancon, C.Z., Dec. 18–22, 1911; at Washington, D.C., Jan. 17 to March 13, 1912). 5 volumes in 2, paged continuously, 1–1127. Printed 1912. *Same* in one volume (House Doc. 680).

House Committee on Naval Affairs

No. 16. Hearings (Dec. 6, 1912–Feb. 19, 1913) . . . . on Estimates Submitted by the Secretary of the Navy, 1913. Printed 1913.

Senate Committee on Interoceanic Canals

No. 17 (57th Cong., 1st sess.). Report on the Proposed Ship Canals through the American Isthmus Connecting the Continents of North and South America, December 1901 (Sen. Report No. 1). (Appendix 22, pp. 493–507: "Maury's Estimate of the Resources of the Gulf of Mexico and of the Caribbean Sea, and of the Importance of Interoceanic Communication, July 2, 1849.") Printed 1901.

No. 18 (59th Cong., 2d sess.). *Investigation of Canal Mat-*

ters. Hearings (Jan. 11, 1906, to Feb. 12, 1907) . . . . in the Matter of the Senate Resolution Adopted January 9, 1906 . . . . 4 volumes paged continuously, 1–3310. Printed 1907. (Sen. Doc. 401.)

No. 19. *Panama Canal* . . . . (Hearings . . . . Jan. 16–23, 1908). Printed 1908.

No. 20 (62d Cong., 2d sess.). *Panama Canal.* Hearings . . . . held at Ancon, Canal Zone, Oct. 26–28, 1911. Printed 1912. (Sen. Doc. 191.)

No. 21 (62d Cong., 2d sess.). *Panama Canal.* Hearings . . . . (March 29 to June 14, 1912) on H.R. 21,969, a Bill to Provide for the Opening, Maintenance, Protection, and Operation of the Panama Canal, and the Sanitation and Government of the Canal Zone. Printed 1912.

COOPER, GEORGE H., REAR ADMIRAL. *Progress of Work on Panama Ship-Canal: Report, March 2, 1883.* Printed 1884. (Sen. Exec. Doc. 123, pp. 1–4, 48th Cong., 1st sess.)

EDMUNDS, GEORGE F., SENATOR. "Joint Resolution (Sen. Res. 122), Dec. 19, 1888," *Congressional Record,* Vol. 20, Pt. 1, p. 338. (50th Cong., 2d sess., Dec. 3, 1888, to Jan. 19, 1889.)

GOETHALS, GEORGE W., LIEUTENANT COLONEL, U.S.A. *The Isthmian Canal.* Printed 1909.

———. *Slides at the Panama Canal.* Printed 1916. (Covers history of slides from 1884 to 1916, with various theories about their causes.)

ISTHMIAN CANAL COMMISSION, 1899–1902. *Report* . . . . *1899–1901* . . . . Printed 1901–1902. 2 volumes. (Sen. Doc. 54, 57th Cong., 1st sess.) Incomplete report.

———. *Same.* Complete in one volume, printed 1904. (Sen. Doc. 222, 58th Cong., 2d sess.)

ISTHMIAN CANAL COMMISSION, 1904–1905. *Proceedings,* March 22, 1904, to March 29, 1905; meetings 1 to 90, with *Circulars* (Nos. 1 to 13, June 25, 1904, to April 3, 1905; *Index*) ; succeeded by *Minutes of Meetings.*

———. *Letter from the Secretary of War* [Jan. 12, 1905], *Transmitting the First Annual Report of the* . . . . *Commission, December 1, 1904* (covering the period March 22 to Nov. 10, 1904). Printed 1905. (House Doc. 226, 59th Cong., 3d sess.)

ISTHMIAN CANAL COMMISSION, 1905–1914. *Annual Report for the Year ending December 1, 1905* (with President Roosevelt's Letter of

Transmittal, Jan. 8, 1906). Printed 1906. (Sen. Doc. 127, Pts. 1–2, 59th Cong., 1st sess.)

    Pt. 1, as above; 440 pp. Illus.

    Pt. 2, *Isthmian Canal,* Message from the President (Jan. 10, 1906) Transmitting Certain Papers to Accompany His Message of January 8, 1906.

ISTHMIAN CANAL COMMISSION, 1905–1914. *Annual Report for the Year ending December 1, 1906.* Printed 1907.

————. *Minutes of Meetings of the Isthmian Canal Commisison and of the Executive and Engineering Committees, April 1905 to March 29, 1914.* Printed from 1905 to 1914. 15 volumes in 4.

    (Beginning with the 91st meeting, April 1905, this publication continues the *Proceedings* of March 22, 1904, to March 29, 1905; Meetings No. 1 to 90.)

————. *General Index, Minutes of Meetings . . . . March 1904 to March 1907* (covering meetings of I.C.C. No. 1 to 122; of its Executive Committee, No. 1 to 24; of its Engineering Committee, No. 1 to 49). Printed 1908.

    An Index (entitled "Panama Canal") to the technical reports of I.C.C. and its committees for the years 1899 to 1914 is embodied in Vol. 2 of *Index to the Reports of the Chief of Engineers, United States Army,* published in 1915–16 as *House Doc. 740* (63d Cong., 2d sess.).

————. *Population and Deaths from Various Diseases in the City of Panama . . . . from November 1883 to August 1906* (pp. 1–16); *Number of Employees and Deaths from Various Diseases among the Employees of the French Canal Companies . . . . from January 1881 to April 1904* (pp. 17–37), Isthmian Canal Commission, Government of the Canal Zone, Health Dept., W. C. Gorgas, Chief Sanitary Officer. Printed 1906.

————. *Report of the Department of Health for the Month of January, 1906,* W. C. Gorgas, Chief Sanitary Officer. Printed 1906.

————. *Sanitary Conditions on the Isthmus of Panama; Reply . . . . to the Report of Dr. C. A. L. Reed,* with letters of the President and Secretary of War in reference thereto. Printed 1905.

    (Contains Dr. Reed's Report to Taft, March 2, 1905, pp. 38–63.)

————. *Catalogue of Equipment, November 1, 1913, Purchased for Use on The Panama Canal and The Panama Railroad between July 1, 1904, and January 1, 1913,* available in Panama Canal Library, Balboa Heights, C.Z.

JOHNSON, EMORY R. *Panama Canal Traffic and Tolls* (Report to Secretary of War, Aug. 7, 1912). Printed 1912.

KIMBALL, WILLIAM W., LIEUTENANT, U.S.N., AND W. L. CAPPS, U.S.N., *Special Intelligence Report on the Progress of the Work on the Panama Canal during the Year 1885.* Printed 1886. (House Misc. Doc. 395, 49th Cong., 1st sess.)

KNOX, PHILANDER C., SENATOR. *Panama Canal,* Speech in the Senate of the United States . . . . June 18, 1906. Printed 1906; reprint from *Congressional Record,* Vol. XL, Pt. 9, pp. 8702–8 (59th Cong., 1st sess.).

NOURSE, JOSEPH E., U.S.N. *The Maritime Canal of Suez from Its Inauguration, November 17, 1869, to the Year 1884;* Prepared under Orders of the Bureau of Navigation, Navy Department. Printed 1884. (Sen. Exec. Doc. 198, 48th Cong., 1st sess.)

PRESIDENT. *A Compilation of the Messages and Papers of the Presidents* . . . . with additional encyclopedic index by private enterprise . . . . New York; Bureau of National Literature, Inc.; prefatory note signed by James D. Richardson. 20 volumes.

RICHARDSON, JAMES D. *Compilation of the Messages and Papers of the Presidents. See* President.

RODGERS, RAYMOND P., LIEUTENANT, U.S.N. *Progress of Work on Panama Ship-Canal:* First Report, Feb. 28, 1883; Second Report, Jan. 27, 1884. Printed 1884. (Sen. Doc. 123, pp. 4–15; 15–25, 48th Cong., 1st sess.)

ROGERS, CHARLES C., LIEUTENANT, U.S.N. *Intelligence Report of the Panama Canal, March 30, 1887.* Printed 1889. (House Misc. Doc. 599, 50th Cong., 1st sess.)

ROOSEVELT, THEODORE, PRESIDENT. *Executive Orders Relating to the Isthmian Canal Commission, March 1904, to June 12, 1911, inclusive.* Printed 1909.

———. *Isthmian Canal,* Message (Feb. 17, 1909) . . . . transmitting Report (Feb. 16, 1909) of the Board of Engineers Appointed to Accompany ex-Secretary of War Taft to the Isthmus . . . . and to Look into the Condition and Safety of the Gatun Dam, etc. Printed 1909. (House Doc. 1458, 60th Cong., 2d sess.)

———. *Special Message . . . . to Congress Concerning the Panama Canal . . . . December 17, 1906.* Printed 1906. (Sen. Doc. 144, 59th Cong., 2d sess.)

STATE DEPARTMENT, *Register . . . . 1876–1878.* Printed 1876–1878.

SULLIVAN, JOHN T., LIEUTENANT, U.S.N. *Report of Historical and Technical Information Relating to the Problem of Interoceanic Com-*

munication by Way of the American Isthmus. By Order of the Bureau of Navigation, Navy Dept. Printed 1883.

SULLIVAN, JOHN T., LIEUTENANT, U.S.N. *Same.* Issued as *House Exec. Doc. 107* (47th Cong., 2d sess.).

TAFT, WILLIAM H., SECRETARY OF WAR. *The Panama Canal* (cover title); Speech . . . . at the St. Louis Commercial Club, St. Louis, Mo. . . . ., November 18, 1905, Washington, D.C., Office of Administration Isthmian Canal Affairs, 1905 (justifying action regarding Wallace).

————. "Secretary Taft's Statement Regarding Mr. John F. Wallace," as printed in the *Washington Post* on June 30, 1905; reprinted, together with Wallace's Letter to Shonts, June 26, 1905, in Congress: *Hearings No. 18,* II, 1362–69 (Sen. Doc. 401, 59th Cong., 2d sess.).

TRIPLER, CHARLES S., SURGEON, U.S.A. "Report of the Regimental Surgeon, Fourth Infantry, to Surgeon General, Sept. 14, 1852," *Sen. Doc. 96,* pp. 454–58 (34th Cong., 1st sess.). Printed 1856; available in Library of Congress and in War College Library.

————. *Same,* in Bullard, Arthur, *Panama, the Canal,* etc., pp. 400–407.

————. *Same,* under the title "Crossing the Isthmus in 1852," *Canal Record,* I, (July 1, 1908), 347–48.

MANUSCRIPTS

Designated in footnotes by (MS).

LIBRARY OF CONGRESS, *Division of Manuscripts,* Washington, D.C.
Taft Papers:
    Taft-Roosevelt ....Boxes II, III
John Barrett Papers.

NATIONAL ARCHIVES, *Legislative Division,* Washington, D.C.
Brown, Robert M. G., Lieutenant, U.S.N.
    Report to the Secretary of the Navy, June 2, 1884, Regarding Progress of Work on the Panama Canal; Transmitted to the Senate January 19, 1885 (48th Cong., 2d sess., Exec.) and 77 Copies Ordered Printed in Confidence for Use of the Senate.

THE PANAMA CANAL, *Archives,* Balboa Heights, C.Z. (P.C. Rec. Bur.)

INDEX

Abbot, Henry L., 67, 76, 101 n.; and Board of Consulting Engineers, 213, 223, 340; member of Comité Technique, 123, 125, 143, 209; quoted, 206
Acquisition Day, May 4, 1904, 133
Adamson, Thomas, 85
"Adriatic," liner, 62
Agua Dulce, 292
Ahorca Lagarto, 15
"Alexander La Valley," crane boat, 319
Alhajuela, 125
Allen, Horatio, 5
Amador, President Manuel, 136, 167, 192, 207, 304; and Roosevelt's visit, 230, 232–33, 235
American Boycott Association, 139
American Committee of the Panama Canal Company, 72
American Contracting and Dredging Company, 72, 73, 109, 119
American Federation of Labor, 185
American Medical Association, 151–52
American Society of Civil Engineers, 57, 105, 138, 343
Ammen, Daniel, 36, 37, 40, 44, 54
Anchorage at Miraflores, 296, 297
Ancon Hospital, 72–73, 121, 133, 140, 142, 234, 282
"Ancon," steamer, 298, 337–38
Anopheles, see Mosquitoes
Appleton, Nathan, 36, 37, 47, 91
Archives of the Panama Canal, x
Army doctor (for sanitary officer), 321
Army engineer (to head Canal), 321, 323; as governor, 325
Army of Panama, the, 268, 273–313
Army, United States: and Canal operation, 321, 323, 325; and regimentation on Isthmus, 264; as solution of Canal problems, 259; see also Army of Panama

Arosemena, Pablo, 93, 207
"Aspinwall," steamer, 12
Aspinwall, town, 14; progress at, 15, 23, 24, 73; see also Colón
Aspinwall, William Henry, 3, 4, 5, 6; town named for, 14
Atlantic terminus of Panama Railroad, 6; see also Limon Bay, Porto Bello
Atrato River, 33, 34, 37

Baggage service, railroad, 16–18, 19
Baïhaut, M., 122
Balboa, 304, 310, 321; see also La Boca
Baldwin, James L., 5, 6, 7, 8, 9
Band, Isthmian Canal Commission, 194, 269, 271
Bangs, Anson M., 252–54
Baratoux, Letellier et Cie., 97, 109
Barbacoas, bridge at, 16, 18, 20, 21, 22; completed, 24, 49; illustration facing 30
Barrett, John, x, 158, 207, 337
Bartlett, Edwin, 5
Bas Obispo, 71, 111, 205, 258, 303
Bates, L. W., 39 n., 211, 213
Battle of the levels, 206–21
Battle of the lockages, 331–37
Battles, Major Ford Lewis, x; poem by, xix
Baudelot, M., 117
Beach, Colonel L. H., 319 n.
Beeks, Gertrude, 279
Bellows, H. W., 59 n.
Bennett, Ira E., 225 n., 278
Benson, E. S., 240
Berges, Aquiles, 121
Bernhardt, Sarah, 98
Bertoncini, C. F., 135
Bierd, W. G., 197, 226, 232, 233, 271–72
Bigelow, John, 59, 60, 92, 102 n.
Bigelow, Poultney, 201–3, 215, 222, 228

Nombre de Dios, 298, 299
Norge, French engineer, 110
North American Dredging Company, 252
Northers, at the Isthmus, 13, 48, 56, 152, 207
Nouailhac-Pioch, French engineer, 110
Nourse, J. E., 45 n.

Obispo, 124; see also Obispo River
Obispo River: and De Lépinay's plan, 40; railroad route along, 5, 22–23; valley, 1
"Ohio," steamer, 16
Old Panama Canal Company, see Compagnie Universelle du Canal Interocéanique de Panama
Oliver and Bangs, 252, 254, 255
Oliver, William J., 252, 254, 255, 257
Opening date of Canal, prospective: 1890, 115; 1891, 110, 112, 127; 1898, 121; 1915, 208, 227, 248, 271, 299, 307, 337–38; 1915 or 1917, 208; Gatun Dam and, 273
"Oregon," U.S.S, 124, 129
Organization plan for Canal: administrative features of, 88–99; construction divisions of, 83, 98, 287, 319; departments of, 321; French company's, 68, 241; under Goethals', 276–79, 282–83, 286–91, 297–98, 321–31; under First Isthmian Canal Commission, 133, 135; under Second Isthmian Canal Commission, 160; Shonts and, 224; Stevens and, 198–99, 204; under Goethals and Canal Zone Government, 330–31; Wallace and, 157, 170
Ossa, San José F. de la, 232, 233 n.
Otis, F. N., 4 n., 5 n., 19 n., 26 n., 27 n.

Pacific Mail Steamship Company, 3
Pacific Terminal, see Port of the Pacific Terminal
Palo Grande, 313

Panamá, 18, 27–28, 42, 46, 47, 49, 55, 214, 236, 262–72; Governor Davis and, 136, 149
Panama Bank, 65
Panama Canal: administrative division of, 98–99; completion of, 40, 43, 62, 63, 65, 72, 83, 88, 90, 95, 103, 107, 109, 110, 121, 141, and see Opening date; Construction divisions of, 83, 98, 109; discontinued under French in 1889, 120; estimated costs of, 40, 43, 44, 45, 56, 57, 63, 65, 107, 281; De Lépinay's plan for, 39–40, 126, 221, 340; Dingler's plan for, 77; first ship transits of, 308, 313; French accomplishment regarding, 125–27; as a frontier, 146; historical epochs of, ix; laborers for, see Laborers, Canal; legal start of, 34; organization and operation of departments for, 321, 330; and Panama Railroad, 4–30, 49, 66, 69; permanent organization for, 319–25; plan of 1898 Commission for, 121, 124–25; profits anticipated from, 38, 44, 63; progress in construction of, 83, 85–86, 89, 95, 97, 98, 99, 100, 103, 105, 107, 108, 109–10 (in 1887), 111–114 (in 1888), 127, 170, 189, 199, 203, 207–8, 248, 281–82, 284, 303, 305, 311, 313; formally proposed, 31; recommended at Paris in 1879, 37; route for, 34; sea-level, see Sea-level canal; single head for, 320–21; specifications for, 45–46, 55, 56, 57, 77; strike of workers on, 71, 278, 307; survey for, 53–57; Totten plan for, 45–46; unit costs of, 143, 203, 207; work discontinued on, 120–21; Wyse and Réclus plan for, 46, 54
Panama Canal Act, 322, 323
Panama Canal Company: bankruptcy of, 105; financial difficulties of, 44–45, 46, 52, 57, 74, 81, 86–87, 89, 102, 103–8, 115–16; financial measures, 42, 43–45, 52,

50746